DISTANCE TO THE GREEN

A caddy's lessons in life, business and golf

by
Gary Abram and Bob O'Byrne

PLAN II **Plan II Publications Limited**
Chicago, Illinois

DISTANCE TO THE GREEN is published by
Plan II Publications Limited, Chicago, Illinois
First Printing, First edition, December, 1996

Printed in the United States of America
Design by D3, Kansas City, MO.
Cover photo and photo on page 173 by Charles Ford, Dallas, TX

All persons are fictional and any resemblance to a real person is
coincidental.

This book is distributed to the trade by—
Scott O'Brien, Inc./Partners Group
P.O. Box 339
Blue Springs, MO 64013-0339
913-676-5010 phone
913-676-5009 fax
800-798-6160 toll free
Visit our Web site at http://www.marketlynx.com/dist2green/

Books are available at quantity discounts when used to promote
products or services.

There are two aspects of *Distance to the Green* that I really appreciated. First, the business philosophy is really valuable and is delivered in a most entertaining way. Secondly, some of my most memorable and rewarding experiences have been as mentor and as protégé. The development of the O'Brien and Scotty relationship is terrific. I look forward to their next book to find out what happens to both.

Rick Darnaby, President of Nutrasweet
Corporate VP/Global Brand Management-Motorola

What a great book! I am reminded that there are no new truths — just life's lessons passed on to others. I am going to share this with my 15-year-old son.

Alan Mauch
Executive Vice President, Employers Reinsurance Corporation

Distance to the Green offers both straightforward and valuable techniques for goal attainment...The lessons ring true not only for anyone starting a new career, but also for anyone who wishes to become more effective and successful. I just wish my putting was as sound as the messages in the book.

Howard E. Jones, Management Consultant
Vice President, Hallmark Cards, Inc. (retired)

This delightful story, set on a golf course, is an instructive and thought-provoking read on some of life's deeper challenges: figuring out where you really want to go and finding the path that will get you there.

Lee Bolman
Henry R. Bloch Leadership Chair, U.of Missouri-Kansas City
Co-author with Terrence Deal, "Leading with Soul"

...it is apparent that the Business World can be offered a great and most comprehensive business learning atmosphere while at the same time enjoy the pleasures of playing and sharing the friendly competition in the best of all games...Golf! You have a winner...

Jon E. Jacobson
Executive Director/CEO Midwest Section PGA

To our most important protégés,
our children and grandchildren,
they make it all worthwhile.

TABLE OF CONTENTS

FOREWORD

Distance to the Green is the culmination of at least 100 hours of mentorship from Bob O'Byrne. About ten years ago, I had the pleasure to work with Bob on an executive search project. Believe me, he was a very different client than any I had ever met. He has a marvelous metaphorical style, sharing insights that I find captivating. Over the years we shared many professional moments. More importantly for me, he found time for long lunches to school me on what was happening in his organization and the challenges it faced. He was always interested in advising me on my own goals and plans. Without a doubt, the business advice he gave me was the most important that I have ever received. It wasn't always what I wanted to hear, but it was always on the mark.

For over 33 years Bob has managed Robert D. O'Byrne & Associates and the Grant Nelson Group in Kansas City, Mo. His companies became the most successful in their niche of any in the Midwest. Anyone who has ever built or managed a company of more than 100 people, especially if those people are very urgent and very talented, knows the challenges. Bob has been a master in building a team, blending all the right elements. My experience with client companies showed me that those skills are incredibly valuable and that Bob's way of expressing those skills is very memorable and rare.

Foreword

As Bob approached retirement, I suggested that our discussions comprised the core of a very interesting treatise on success (not only business success, because much extended outside the business world). I knew that these ideas, principles and concepts (Bob calls them bromides) would be valuable to others like myself, but that very few people have the good fortune to have access to a mentor like Bob. So Bob and I set about the very fun task of recapturing the flavor of many discussions covering the past ten years, including additional elements that he has developed, refined and successfully implemented during his career.

As we composed this narrative about a mentor and a protégé, I was struck by the timelessness of Bob's advice. This is not cutting edge "new think." It is tried and true advice honed over a lifetime, based on real world experience, not academic musings. We offer sound principles and bromides that worked for a man as he built a successful life and career.

I was fortunate to pass his way. Co-authoring this book was a breeze when you have the sort of content Bob provides. We would not have accomplished it without the help and advice of many, many others, most especially the wordsmithing by Lisen Tammeus who helped structure and compose the narrative.

Gary Abram

DISTANCE to the GREEN

DISTANCE TO THE GREEN

A caddy's lessons in life, business and golf

"On your deathbed you will have total consciousness.
I got that goin' for me."
Carl, the Greenskeeper, from Caddyshack

The summer before my senior year in college, I was Scotty, the looper, the caddie. Most people would say I grew up in a suburb outside of Chicago. That's only partly true. I was raised there. I really grew up at National Golf Club. This is a diary of that summer.

My full name is David Alvin Scott. That summer it was just Scotty. Scotty do this, Scotty do that. Yes, sir, Mister Johnson. Yes, ma'am, Miz Weidersham. Be glad to, Dr. Geezel.

My sentence to loop at the National Golf Club was just that...indentured servitude. My college golf coach, Coach Robertson, had had enough of me. But he saw something in me, I guess, that made him want to give me one last chance. So he gave me an ultimatum for the summer: Go caddie and learn or don't bother to tee it up for the fall golf season. At the time, I was more than slightly mystified why Coach Robbie would threaten me, his number two player, with the loss of my scholarship. (Number one was a pretty fair striker who later had some success on the tour with a couple of top 10 finishes, including a sudden death playoff loss to a fellow named Lanny at the Andy Williams, or Sammy Davis, or Danny Thomas back when tournaments had people's rather than corporate names). Robertson's basic message was: "Dave, you are a helluva player, but you are the most stubborn, uncoachable kid I've ever had here in 23 years of coaching." Of course, I didn't know what he was talking about. As usual, I hadn't paid too much attention to his earlier, more subtle admonitions. But this got through to me in a big way. Golf was the most important thing in my life.

Coach Robbie proceeded to inform me that he had arranged my summer and that I was to report to an old college bud of his, Richard Nelson, at the "caddyshack" of the National Golf Club.

National and Rich Nelson turned out to be two of the grandest institutions in the world, but at that particular moment I was truly angry. I had planned a summer of girls, rock'n'roll, and hustling some gandies on some of the local courses for $25 Nassaus. Robbie had other plans for me. "Report the day after Memorial Day to National, or it's been nice knowing you."

It was painfully obvious from Robbie's tone that if I had any thought of playing for him on the golf team then I was going to National and I'd better return with an adjusted attitude. You see, I fancied myself as a player, but that summer I learned that I wasn't even close. I sure as hell didn't see myself as a caddie, but on June 1, I began the greatest education of my life while a novice caddie at National.

National is 178 of the most beautiful acres on this planet. For a golfer, it is heaven. Everything about your golf experience at National is stellar. From the moment you pull through the gates, the treatment you receive is the essence of class. As a caddie, however, my position on the food chain did not allow me the same deferential treatment. In fact, caddies were only allowed to play on

Mondays when the course was closed and after we had finished our other chores. Robbie had indeed sentenced me to purgatory: He had sent a golfaholic to one of golf's hallowed grounds and made him carry the bags of the rich and famous, whose golf swings were generally brutal, while limiting my play to once a week — maybe.

You can imagine my attitude when I reported for my first loop at the caddyshack. Oh, yeah, "caddyshack" is a tad off-base. Nothing at National resembles a shack. The trash receptacles at National are made of marble and brass. And my boss, the caddy-master, Rich Nelson, was one of the world's classiest guys. He was silver-haired senatorial, with all the aura that came with it: bushy eyebrows, impeccable dress, the slight corpulence of a man of success and the worldliness to make him comfortable amongst kings and the titans of industry. Everyone at National had a nickname except Rich. It just wouldn't have been right to call him anything else. He had been a super successful insurance executive, a yachtsman and bon vivant. I asked him once why he was hanging out with a bunch of reprobates like us. He merely winked and said, "Hey, it's a good summer job."

Well, I thought it was anything but a good summer job and he knew it. So he sent me off with a foursome that included a big Irishman named Bob O'Brien.

That day O'Brien changed my life so profoundly that to this day I am astounded by how he was able to do it in four hours on the golf course. It wasn't one of those lightening bolt kind of deals, but he got into my head that day and by the end of the summer you wouldn't have recognized me.

DISTANCE to the GREEN

JUNE 2

Meeting My Mentor

The sun came up gloriously that morning, and for a moment I had sublimated my godawful attitude. I was going to give this my best effort. Breakfast was served to the caddies over in the shack at 6:30 and I got a chance to meet my fellow loopers. God, what a collection. There were a few indentured servants like myself, college boys, but most were grizzled veterans with names like Squeaky, Goose, Conehead, Bogie and Snake-Eyes. First lesson: Never, ever try to keep up with these guys if they are drinking, playing cards or telling lies. Just sit back and watch them, warily, because I tell you, this breed would eat their young.

We newbies would be sprinkled in with the vets to apprentice. Now I know I could've outplayed any of those veterans, but I had a lot to learn about many things and caddying was one of them.

Rich Nelson must have intuitively known that when he put me into O'Brien's foursome. Until that morning, I had always taken the path of least resistance and called it my destiny. I was very good at a number of things. In fact, I was beyond "very good" in a few things. But I was a non-starter in almost everything that didn't come to me quickly. If I could feature a talent or skill, I was there. But if it didn't happen right off, I bailed. Consequently, I came to believe that I was damn good at almost everything and those things I couldn't accomplish weren't worth messing with anyway. I had rationalized much of the known world away and along the way eliminated my need for teachers, coaches and mentors. This retarded my learning curve, big time. In my universe, if I wasn't gifted in some way in an endeavor, the whole activity was deemed worthless and satisfying only for those hapless souls who didn't appreciate the really important things in life.

Later, I realized that Coach Robbie must have gotten to Rich Nelson early because Rich made it his mission to have me caddie for some of the greatest teachers I could have had. That summer I got my masters in both life and business, although on June 2, I was mostly trying to figure out a way to get back home, catch up with my buddies, and still preserve my scholarship and place on the golf team.

National is an incredible place. Not only is it architecturally, topographically and botanically one of the wonders of the civilized world, it is "ground zero" for meeting most of the powerful people of the industrialized world. National is a club that requires wealth to belong, but wealth itself cannot get you a place at the table. You have to be asked to join. The club has 400 members, worldwide. Those 400 members and their guests make up a who's who of the Fortune 1000, world politics, the arts and entertainment — the Hollywood types — and the generally rich and famous.

Now Rich Nelson knew, and Coach Robbie knew, and little ol' Scotty was about to learn that if Scotty — whose major short fall was that he apparently had been born with the inability to listen — paid attention, he would be privy to the secrets of the universe.

That morning when I picked up O'Brien's bag, I was still a member of the deaf and dumb society, but that was about to change.

Bob O'Brien was 55 years old the morning I picked up his bag to walk the 18 finest holes I had ever seen. National is a par 72, 6,672 yards from the white tees, slope rating from there is 139.

A pretty tough track, but nothing like what they can set up from the Champ tees: 7,134 yards of peril, sloped at 148. If they double cut the greens, you'd best bring balls with teeth...it will eat your lunch. Nobody plays back there except scratch golfers and pros brought in for corporate deals. It was common that summer to see a leading PGA player come in for the day and pick up a check for $20,000 to smooze with the heavies of industry and smoke some 1-irons past the weekend hackers who pay big bucks to rub shoulders with the pros.

I carried O'Brien's bag six times that summer. Because National's membership generally lives in other parts of the country, I never carried anyone else's bag more than once. Ms. Sara Dawson, one of the few female members of National, kept requesting me but Richard, noting the gleam in Ms. Dawson's eye, conveniently saw that I was busy during the time Ms. Dawson was scheduled. Too bad for me because Sara was generous in every way and an excellent tipper.

Tips are the world monetary system for loopers. National paid minimum wage. No benefits. Three squares and a dorm-type set up for caddies who were non-locals. Some of the vets were family guys who had moonlighting situations in the off-season and lived in town.

Given the great weather and the opportunity to make two loops per day, you could make some fairly serious coin in a summer. All cash. The other passion around the club was the gentlemanly wager. The vets had created a highly imaginative book that allowed for wagering on almost everything. It stopped just short of the proverbial bet on which of two birds would leave its perch first.

During those six rounds with Bob O'Brien, I got to know him pretty well. After all, we had communed with nature for about 25-plus hours and I had gotten to see many facets of the man. It is true that sports — especially golf — does not build character, it reveals it.

However, at 8:38 a.m. on June 2, I knew nothing of the man or the journey I was about to embark upon. O'Brien was a big guy. Now I am tall for a golfer, 6'-4", but O'Brien with his overall size and bearing just struck me right off as a guy who in his younger days (or even now) you wouldn't mess with.

The great attitude I had with the dawning of the new day had been supplanted by the realization that I was a lowly caddie conscripted into a band of hard livin' gamblers. This was going to be my boot camp and by its nature not intended to be my idea of fun. I was too big to cry, but I had this overwhelming sensation that the day was going to be about 62 hours long and by the end of summer I would resemble a sort of a modern day Oliver Twist or Dead End Kid. The end of the innocence.

The gloom swept over me as I shouldered Bob's bag. A quiet resolution of my fate surfaced as sullenness.

Bob, on the other hand, was a celebrant of life. He had slain many dragons, drunk the nectar of the gods, seen the seven wonders, and he had no use for a punk looper with an attitude.

Bob O'Brien did not get to the top of his field by letting others dictate the agenda and, by God, on this glorious day I was not going to contribute any vibes that weren't positive. He let me slide on the 1st hole when I performed my caddie duties perfunctorily, but his antenna started picking up my signals as we walked up the 2nd fairway.

He must have assumed I was shy or intimidated because he began to try to draw me out, asking where I was from, what college, my major, the typical line of inquiry that you get used to as a college student. I have since learned many things about Bob, but two were quickly apparent. One, he had a very sensitive antenna and could size up a situation instantly. Two, if he wanted a piece of you, he was not ever going to back off. And that day, for whatever reason, he saw me as a project and dogged my sorry rear end the rest of the day. I was too stupid to see the great compliment he was paying me, but later I came to realize that Bob never has the energy or time to spend on anyone or anything that he doesn't care about.

So the questions came. What did I think about this or that? Not anything to do with golf. If he had asked me to read a putt or which club to use, that would have been a relief. No, he was sizing me up. Although at the time, I just thought he was playing with me like a cat with a mouse. I was totally and utterly overmatched. This guy was a PLAYER in the true sense of the word, and in the wide world of life, I really was just a caddie. But God knows why Bob saw in me more than that. Maybe he saw some of himself in me or some weird need to share. But I am thankful, whatever the reason.

When we reached the clubhouse, yet another monstrously important moment occurred. Bob stiffed me. Yep, no tip. I was dumbstruck.

"Scotty, I enjoyed our stroll," he said. "This is the time when I usually tip my caddie $50, but I won't insult you with money, Scotty. Nope, I am going to give you another chance tomorrow. See if you can't come out on the course with the right attitude. When I come to the National, I expect my caddie to share in the sublime nature of this place. (I had to look up sublime, which means outstanding spiritual or moral worth.) Today I asked you a bunch of questions; tomorrow I am going to tell you some things that I think have greater value than the paltry $50 I might have given you. I'll let Richard know that I want you to tote my bag tomorrow. Seven o'clock sharp."

With that, he headed off to the locker room leaving me standing there with my mouth open wide.

DISTANCE to the GREEN

JUNE 3

Goal Attainment: Wiring the Deal

How different the world can look in just 24 hours. I had no idea what was going to happen, but my attitude was very different. I don't think I could have verbalized the change but something was going on in my head. I had even gotten over the fact that the sunburn and blisters I earned the day before had gone monetarily unrewarded. The static I was getting from Squeaky and Goose would have bothered me yesterday, but today I was moving off into a new universe where their hazing was insignificant.

Rich told me to grab Mr. O'Brien's bag and go to the 1st tee. So off I went to Club Storage, picked up a pin placement sheet, shouldered Bob's bag and headed that way. Rich and Dutch, the greenskeeper, had devised a pin placement sheet. It was a daily crib sheet for the caddies, so that we would know exact distances to the pins from almost anywhere on the golf course. A good caddie is like a good hack or cabbie in London. He has to know every little street and lane in the city. So it is with good caddies. They should know every distance to the front of the green, the back of the green and to the pins. Each day, Dutch would provide Rich with a schematic of the pin placements on each hole. This was before the days of relatively inexpensive copiers, but Rich had found an old mimeograph machine in one of his district offices when he retired. So he set it up in the Club Storage area and each day we could pick up the placement of the hole measured from the front of the green.

It really gave us the illusion of knowing every inch of the course. We all carried a yardage book of the course in our back pocket although most of the veteran caddies rarely needed or used it. Occasionally, they'd bring it out like they do on television and brandish it like it was being consulted. But the guys who had been there for years knew the distances from every angle and shot on the course.

Bob knew the course very well and rarely asked me for yardage, or "mileage," as he called it. But many members played so infrequently that they always needed to know. They rarely chose the right club on their own even with the correct distances. A good caddie, a trusted caddie, does more than give the distance. He also suggests the club for the player. After watching a player for a few holes, a trained eye can assess the skill level and the average distance that the player will hit a given club. So if it is 155 yards to the pin, a power player can hit with a 9-iron but a weaker player needs a wood. A good caddie blends good club advice while keeping the player's ego intact. A "macho" player is always pushing his clubs, trying to get more distance out of the club than he should expect. So he overswings, miss-hits the ball and wonders why his 7-iron doesn't go as far as Freddie Couples' does. O'Brien, on the other hand, played it just the opposite. He was very strong but never one to overswing. He wanted to swing as slowly as possible and get a pure hit on the ball. Consequently, he got terrific results.

Bob was alone and it appeared no one else was joining us.

"Hey, Scotty. It's just you and me, my boy. I told Richard I had to catch an early flight out and I wanted to play solo so we could move right along. I'm off to Vegas with my friend Charlie and probably won't be back up here until next month. In the meantime, I want to leave you with some food for thought. Let me tell you a story."

He fished his monogrammed balls and tees out of the side pocket of his bag, yanked on his glove and prepared to tee off. No fanfare, no dramatic pre-shot routine. Just getting down to business. I loved it.

Number 1 at National is really strong. Most golf course architects start you off with a par 4. Generally there won't be a lot of trouble — sort of a warm-up hole. The architect knows that most players are not mentally or physically ready for a tough hole. Besides, a tough hole backs up the golf course at the 1st tee. The golf experience is going to be more pleasant if everyone has a chance to move smartly off tee Number 1. Having said that, National is the opposite. The course was built 65 years ago. It has always been an exclusive national golf club and a concern about a traffic jam at the 1st tee was never a priority.

Members and guests have cursed Number 1 since day one. Three factors make it tough. First, it is long — 427 yards — and made longer in that it is uphill. The elevation change from tee to green is 128 feet. Secondly, the hole faces the south into the prevailing southerly breeze that blows all summer long. The third factor is that the green is really too small. Legend has it that the nurseryman who supplied the seed and sod for the original construction got into an argument with the architect. The architect said he still owed him but the nurseryman said that he had fulfilled the contract and wasn't going to start giving away his profit. Back and forth they went for days like two stubborn mules. Every green was in except Number 1 and the club founder was getting very impatient. He wanted everything in and perfect for the inaugural invitational tournament. So he ordered the architect to redesign the green, assuring him that they would rebuild it in the fall to the original specs. Although the members hated shooting at that postage stamp, it never was rebuilt.

O'Brien was not a golfer who needed the customary deadly silence to play. He had great concentration and would even talk while he was in his backswing. "I grew up in a little town in Oklahoma — Shawnee, Oklahoma, to be exact. One of the things we used to do when we had the money was to go to the movies — an afternoon matinee. There was always a serial where some guy was thrown off of a cliff at the end. But he wasn't dead, otherwise we wouldn't have a serial next week. The movie heroes were usually cowboys who sang but never touched girls, or maybe a cowboy with a bunch of ne'er-do-wells hanging around him. This was the 1930s. I was seven, maybe eight years old.

"Whenever we would come out of the movie, we would be in the mood of whatever the movie had been. We became the hero and it was make-believe. We could ride with the wind. Our draw was so fast no one could see our hands move. We were whomever the hero had been. Roy Rogers or whomever.

"One particular movie day we got out and we were buzzing with total energy. Ready to take on the world. But we all had to go home. So everybody split off and went home. But I was still feeling the buzz of excitement from the movie.

"I was walking alone and the rest of the kids were going toward their own houses and I saw this guy standing on the corner under a streetlight. It was dusk. I don't know why but I wanted to sneak up on this guy. So I ran around behind the back of this house — I knew the neighborhood — and snuck and crawled on my belly (I didn't need to, of course). But I finally got within about 15 feet of his back.

"I think he probably had a date and was working up the courage to go knock on his girlfriend's door. He was smoking a cigarette and waiting for the proper time to show up. I didn't know the guy — he looked kind of geeky, actually. I walked up behind him and I put my knuckles against his back. I remember thinking that my finger wasn't gonna feel about like a gun because it was little. So I used my two front knuckles and I put 'em in the middle of his back and I said 'Stick 'em up.'

"And God, this guy put his hands up and said, 'Don't hurt me.' This power surge went through me. I said, 'Oh, I won't hurt you. You got any money?' He said, 'I don't have any money.' I said, 'Well, you sure you don't have any money?' He said, 'I don't have any money!' So I said, 'OK, take off running and don't look back.' This guy took off running and he didn't look back. And I went home.

"That was the first time I ever had the total feeling of control, power, adrenaline — all of those things that you really don't get very often."

In the course of telling this tale, Bob had smoked a driver, then a 3-iron to the green. The hole, like most in the world, is not so tough if you can hit it long and straight, and on this particular occasion Bob was both. He was still 10 feet off the green, but right in front so his approach to the pin would be a chip with his 8-iron.

"The next time I remember feeling that power was during the war and my folks worked at the Eudora gun powder ammunition factory. Then they moved to Kansas City for different jobs and left us four kids in Baldwin with my grandparents. We were going to school there. Not a real good deal. She was working at North American. He was working at Pratt and Whitney. We were down on the God-forsaken farm.

"Now, I knew their address in Kansas City, but I'd never been there. One weekend I decided I'd go. It was 1943 and I was 10 years old. I hopped on the Trailways bus and went to Kansas City. Took the streetcar and I found the address where they were living — I knew about where it was. I got there and knocked on the front door and this lady answered the door. She was not my mother. I said, 'I'm looking for my mother.' She said, 'Who's your mother?' I said, 'Mrs. O'Brien.' She looked at me and she said, 'You're her son? I thought you were down in Baldwin.' I said, 'Well, I came up to spend the day with her.' I could tell something was wrong. She said, 'She's around in back. Go through the garage.'"

Bob had chipped the ball to about six feet from the hole, but as his story about his parents unfolded, I could see it visibly effecting him. He couldn't get comfortable over the putt as he spoke. In fact, he backed off several times, as if he were trying to get the correct line for the putt.

"So I walked around — the garage door was open and there were my mother and father living behind the furnace. Not a good idea. My father saw me and started crying because he was embarrassed. Here I was, 10 years old, and here they were living behind a furnace. All they had was a bed and old metal shelving and their clothes were just sitting up on the shelf. Their bathroom, if they had to go, really was upstairs. But he was using the drain on the washing machine as a urinal. Something like that can leave you with a long-term sense of 'not me.'"

He missed the first putt, badly pushing it to the right. He left himself 18 inches but above the hole.

"I just felt the whole scene was unacceptable. Not because 'I'm too good for it.' It's just that it wasn't right. It was not acceptable. I made a pact with myself at that moment that I wasn't going to live like that. Ever.

"I remember my dad became a true alcoholic about that time. God knows he had reason. Somehow though, he managed to get us all back together in Kansas City, so all six of us were together. We were living with a preacher and his wife."

He missed the second putt and tapped in for a double bogey. It was the only time all summer I saw him putt like that.

"It was supposed to be an example to the whole church of the preacher's godliness and generosity. But it immediately became clear to me that my mother was his wife's scullery maid. She was treating the whole family like we were white trash. The Harvest Queen of Oklahoma Baptist University was scrubbing toilets. Once during that time I came upon the preacher's wife berating my mother. She just took it. She was afraid that we'd all get kicked out.

"But that wasn't in my mind. I went up to the lady. I wasn't as big as she was, but close. And I remember pushing her. I said, 'If you ever talk to my mother like that again, I'm gonna hit you. Don't ever, ever talk to my mother like that again.' She said, 'You can't talk to me like that, you're just a child.' I said, 'I'm a child, but I'm not a fool.' She said, 'Then just get out of here.' And I said, 'We're gone.' So my dad came home that night and I had everything all packed up. And we took off. We slept in the car that night."

As we approached the 2nd tee, he flipped me his ball so I could clean it. I finally got up the nerve to break in, "You were homeless?"

"We were homeless. But not for long. We rented a house. That's not the point. When you go through those experiences, they don't go away easy. You learn very quickly that you're not willing to let things pass that you normally would because you know they 'shoot horses.' That's where that expression comes from. Have you heard it?"

I shook my head no. Part of me wanted to remind this guy I was just his caddie, the one he hadn't tipped yesterday. But I was feeling silly and cowardly for not having one intelligent thing to say. "They shoot horses," he said. "They were willing, whoever they were, to drive my father into the ground. They were willing to make a scullery maid out of my mother. They didn't care. They'd do whatever it took because they didn't care. Not me."

By this point in his story, I had said about as many words as the number of strokes Bob had taken. He was 2 over par after five holes. During the rest of the front 9 all I could think about was that little kid putting his finger in some guy's back — although I had real trouble picturing O'Brien as a ratty seven year old.

My brother and I used to play Batman and Robin. We'd "fly" across the room, wearing Mom's sheets or good table cloths as capes and balancing our hips on the edge of the couch, bodies stretched out and arms stiff. We sort of knew we weren't Batman and Robin — Mom beat that into our heads and our behinds. But we had this sense that we could be if we practiced "flying" enough and if we emulated their every word and action.

As I picked the dirt clods out of my "nails," it hit me. O'Brien had made me realize that I had just plain accepted that I couldn't be Robin. Okay, well, not Robin. But I had lost or put aside whatever guts a seven year old has to have to be whoever the hell he wants to be and do what he wants to do.

Of course, by the time O'Brien was 10 he had seen some stuff and pulled some stunts that would make most of us cower. Some people tell those "back when I was a dumb and fearless kid" stories as cocktail party amusements. Most guys at National have that kind of lore — mostly of when they were freewheeling teens or frat boys. But O'Brien told his stories in a different way. No regret or self-criticism, no bragging or false machismo. I knew that he hadn't changed very much. He'd do the same things he'd done then. I wondered how many people could say that. I couldn't, but now I wished that I could.

The conversation during the rest of the front 9 was considerably lighter in subject matter. He had been so honest and frank that we needed some relief before we ventured back into that realm. So we talked sports and golf and cars and other manful things that guys talk about when they need a break from intimacy.

We made the turn in 94 minutes. The pace at which a man plays the game of golf is usually the pace he lives his life. With O'Brien, it was quick, decisive, and direct. More than once Bob used a gesture that I have since used many, many times. He would turn his hand on its side like a karate chop, squint one eye like he was sighting down his forearm and then bring his arm down in manner that indicated that we were going straight ahead, right now, and we were not going waver one bit from our course. It was emphatic and confident. When you saw that motion, you knew which way to go.

That summer Bob told me much about his life growing up, but on the back 9 that morning he laid out a formula for me that positively changed the way I looked at the world and my place in it.

Up until that point, I was just among that "mass of men living a life of quiet desperation." Bob liked to use that quote by Thoreau. And he was right. Most people, me included, perceive the game of life as one of defensive struggle, reaction. O'Brien was without a doubt an offensive player. He was always ready to go for the score.

On the 11th hole at National, he commenced a lesson on goal attainment that would have the same impact on me as if I had stumbled across the original tablets of the Ten Commandments. I am sure Moses would have enjoyed the 11th because he's probably the only one who could have successfully handled the water hazards on that mother of a hole.

Eleven is a 445-yard, par 4. The tee shot has to carry 225 yards over the first lake. The second lake surrounds the green. That summer the contractor who dove the lake pulled 3,250 golf balls from those two lakes.

As Bob pushed his tee through the plush zoysia of the 11th, he turned his head to me and asked, "So, Scotty, what brings you here to National? I saw you killing the ball over on the practice range last night. You should be playing, not loop-ratting."

Ah, I thought. A sympathetic soul. I was about to agree with him when he quickly continued, "Yes, to be your age again. If I knew then what I know now..."

That emboldened me. "Mr. O'Brien, what would you do if you could go back to my age?"

"Scotty, I wouldn't change a thing. I have no regrets. I benefited from my mistakes as much as I was damaged by my successes. However, if you are interested, I'll reveal a few of my bromides, which might steepen your learning curve."

I wasn't real sure what all that meant, but if the wisdom of a National member could guide me down a similar path, I was game.

He continued, "Scotty, where are you headed? What are your goals? If you're one of rare breed that can answer that question, how're you going to get there? Why go there at all? What tools will you need to get there?"

Whoa, Bob, I thought, where is there? Obviously, I didn't have a clue, so I fell back to safe ground. "Mr. O'Brien, if you play your fade, I would aim this shot towards those traps on the left."

"Scotty, when I was a little younger than you are now, I became a truth seeker. And over long hours of debate and discussion with a friend, we arrived at a formula that has gone through much refinement and validation over the years. If you'd like, I can lay it out for you."

Bob's tee shot started out just over the edge of the water, cut smartly over the traps which I had suggested as a target, and settled to earth, right in the middle of the fairway. He had set up his approach perfectly, which would be a 3-iron from about 185 to a pin cut on the front right of the two-tiered green on 11.

As I handed Bob his 3-iron, I opened the door to enrichment, the import of which I could not contemplate at that time. "Sure, let 'er rip."

"Scotty, if I could give you one insight, it would be the formula to goal attainment. It is the essence of success. It's the ability to reach a goal, to win. On the surface it is deceptively simple, yet most people don't have a clue about this. They confuse success with kismet, chance and luck. Some wind up on third base thinking they have hit a triple, only later to be undone because they shortcut the formula. Luck has no stamina. My formula does.

"The formula has five parts, and each is equally important. To leave out any step is fatal to the process. Scotty, this isn't academic. I use this all the time. Constantly. It is not contrived, although I probably use it less now than in the early years of building my business, because people tend to get the hell out of the way. You know, who wants to go to war over nothing?

"**Step One: Define**. What is it that you want to accomplish? What is your goal? What needs to be resolved? You cannot start this process without a clear definition of what you want to accomplish. Remember that each of the five parts of goal attainment are equally vital. That goes for step one. Really give some thought as you define your goal. It might be a very simple goal or very, very complex one. Regardless, you do NOT have a goal until you can define it, until you know what you want to do."

Bob parred Number 11 during the recitation of step one. His 3-iron had landed just to the right of the green, about seven feet off. For a big guy, he had a deft touch with his wedge and got up-and-down finishing with a six-foot putt.

Number 12 is a par 3 over the same lake that forms the hazard in front of 11. This tricky little devil is only 132 yards from the back tees, but the green is exceptionally narrow. This places a premium on accuracy with large, deep bunkers all around and water in front that swallows a short tee shot.

"Eight-iron, Scotty. **Step two** is just as vital as the others. I call it the smell test. **The smell test** asks this very important question: Is it right that you accomplish your goal? Don't go trying to be a bully and get something done that won't stand the smell test. If somebody wants you to solve a problem for them that is not right to be solved, pass. Say no! So you have to determine if this is something that is right to be accomplished. This is the "why" part of goal attainment. Does it feel right? Because if it doesn't, you won't make the commitment. No way will you follow through."

"Now, Scotty, I warned you that this formula appears simple and it really is, but you would be amazed how often I have seen people sully themselves in pursuit of their goals. They left their moral, or ethical, or spiritual homebase in pursuit of whatever. They either lost their compass or never had one. How many times have we seen the rich and the famous mess in their nest and become one of the fallen? One day they are on the cover of the big deal magazine, next we read of them in the newspaper filing Chapter 11 or plea bargaining with the prosecutor. Scotty, frankly, it's one of the reasons I've always kept a low profile with the press. Pride cometh before the fall, Scotty, me boy. Each of these steps is equally important as the other. If you leave out any one of them…if you don't know precisely what it is you want done, you're in trouble because you're just wandering around blasting. If you don't know if it'll pass the smell test, you could get shot down because it's not right. You'll know when something isn't right with your olfactory system. If you even have a nagging doubt that something can't pass the smell test, it's probably even worse than you think.

Don't try to trick your nose. Pass."

O'Brien hit a beautiful knock down 8-iron into 12. When it left his club, I feared the bank in front of the green might grab and throw it into the soup, but instead it caught the front of the green, took one big hop and threw on the brakes to stop 12 feet from the hole. His putt for birdie was going to be a slippery right to left breaker. O'Brien's approach to the game was very straight-forward. He took little time reading the green or standing over the ball. He claimed that slow play ranked with income taxes, mosquitoes and all viruses as the banes of modern existence.

"Step three," he began just as his birdie fell into the cup, "and this is critical: **Find the path.** See a way to get it done. It might be convoluted, it might be multi-faceted but have a blueprint. Let's say your goal is to go to Chicago. It could be right to go to Chicago, but without a path, you might end up in San Francisco.

"This part of the process is the cool logic of it. And I mean cool. You must give yourself enough intellectual distance to see if the goal can be accomplished. This requires visualizing a set of doable and controllable actions that lead to the accomplishment of your goal."

Hole 13 at National is a favorite of the pros who play the course. It is a "decision" hole that rewards or punishes depending on the decision and execution. Par 5,496 yards. That's a short par 5 for most of the pros, whose drives are typically 270 to 300 yards. That means a 4-to 6-iron second shot for most of them, so if they hit the green they are putting for eagle. However, 13 has a creek right in front and a kidney-shaped green that is slick as asphalt, really severe from back to front. So if you're past the hole or over the back of the green, you can easily 3 putt. So what are the golfer's options? Put the creek in play or lay up and try to wedge it close to the pin. I don't know if it was the discussion of Chicago or San

Francisco that distracted him but Bob hit his drive towards Baltimore. Into the lumber yard. Out of bounds.

Unfazed, he reloaded and hit his next tee shot right down the middle, about 295 yards. "Always easier the second time. Finding the path is the strategy part of goal attainment. But if you have done a good job of defining the goal, and the goal passes the smell test, then the path is more easily found. Study your path carefully. Ready, fire, aim won't work. See the path all the way to the finish. Study the path. Let me really try to drive this point home: Without the path you should not proceed. If your path is dotted with land mines then you will invariably blow your leg or other body parts off. If you can afford to lose a leg or something, go on ahead. Me, I like my parts too much to head down that sort of path. Consider every aspect of the path, then move to step four."

Bob was lying 3 because of the penalty for the ball out of bounds. He was very competitive and very decisive. It took him about three milliseconds to decide that from there he was going to go for it. I knew what his goal was: par. I knew he thought it passed the smell test and he told me his path: "Five-iron, Scotty."

Evidently, Bob was a little too pumped for that club because he airmailed the 5-iron over the green, with the ball settling in a swale behind the putting surface. Now the fun would begin, because as good a wedge player as Bob was, he would have great difficulty getting up and down from there.

"Step four: Commit! This is the one that most people find extremely difficult. I don't mean to commit in some kind of phony, best effort kind of way. Best efforts could mean anything. Actually they mean less than anything. They mean nothing. The old college try. Commit in the sense that you're going to put as many chips on the table as it takes to get to Chicago. All the chips you have, if necessary. No one can compete with that.

"I'm talking about a willingness to put it all on the line. So that nothing that comes along can deter you from your commitment. Scotty, the first three steps are conceptual. There are millions of success stories concocted in the fantasy world until you get to number four: commit. Lots of guys have good intentions, great business plans, smart guys, rich guys. But step four is about character and strength and passion and belief. This is where many a well-laid plan collapses: at the commitment level. I can honestly say that I've met my match a few times, but no one has ever exceeded my level of commitment. When I make a commitment, I know that the only thing between me and the attainment of my goal is time."

Well, Bob had a commitment to finish Number 13 and, as I feared, the green would not hold his flop wedge and it trickled to the front of the green. He was fortunate to 2-putt for a double bogey, 7.

A seven, a hockey stick, would have sent me over the edge, but Bob shrugged it off. I recalled his admonition for me to revel in the sublimity of the game and the moment, and I realized that what was a golfing calamity to me was not perturbing to him. I took a deep breath for both of us, happened to notice a hawk circling above searching for brunch and that a gentle breeze was keeping us perfectly comfortable. I was "there," but until that moment I really didn't know where "there" had been or that " there" was there all the time. I was beginning to undergo a transformation.

The tee box for Number 14 and step five arrived simultaneously. Fourteen is sort of a let up hole. The course lets you get back up on your feet before it beats the heck out of you on the finishing holes. Fourteen is a straight-forward, par 4,426-yarder. The fairway has two traps on both sides of the fairway that need to be avoided. The fairway is relatively wide between them, however, about 36 yards. If the hole is going to hurt you, it will be in those bunkers or on the green, which is one of the largest on the golf course.

I handed Bob his driver and he promptly spanked his Titleist about 275, again favoring the right side of the fairway because of his slight fade. He flipped me his club and we resumed our lesson. **"Step five is pass go. Start.** Don't let this turn into what I call 'beer talk' where people sit around and big time themselves over all the big deals they're gonna do. So, action. Commence. Start."

I must have had a stupid look on my face when I remarked, "Just start?"

"Yeah, Scotty, just start."

I repeated myself, "Just start."

"Scotty, I told you this was simple stuff. But you know what? This may be the hardest part of the formula. You can't believe how many people blink when they face their dreams, their goals, their future, themselves. Usually you see them retreat back into analytics. That's the safe harbor for the uncommitted. Stay near shore and talk about goals."

Bob had an easy 7-iron to the green as he continued, "Many goals don't require gut level, deep down, soul searching commitment. So the 'pass go' part is no big deal. However, the things that really matter, after you have defined the goal, passed the smell test, seen the path and made the commitment, passing go can be terrifying, debilitating and paralyzing. But once 'go' is passed, the commitment must take over. You have got to bet the pot to win the pot."

"No bluffing, right?"

"Now you've got it, Scotty! You're really learning. The best way to bluff — the magnificent way to bluff — is not to be bluffing. That's what I am talking about here — I am not bluffing. I am committed and I am going all the way. It's fixed. It's wired...I am not going to lose. So there's no bluff at all. When I go through the goal attainment process and decide to pass go, I am going to succeed."

This sounded unreal, impossible. A sure-fire way to success? How could that be?

"Mr. O'Brien, what if it can't be done?"

Then he hit me with it. The honest-to-God secret to success. So incredibly plain that after all these years it still flabbergasts me that I hadn't seen it before. But in retrospect, I have seen that so many other people didn't have the secret either.

"Scotty, if you can't wire the deal, if it has any chance of not working, don't go to the dance, my friend. Do NOT go."

"Don't go?"

"Right. If it isn't wired, do NOT go."

"How do you know if you've got it wired?"

"Oh, the security is there to behold."

"What if it's complicated and full of problems?"

"Maybe it can be wired, but I can't wire it."

"Then?"

"Don't go. Happens all the time. I've been in deals where I couldn't find the competitive edge to get it wired, so I didn't go. A month later I think, oh wow, here was a way to do it. Now the opportunity has passed. Happens all the time. The ability to say no and stick with it is crucial.

"Remember earlier when I quoted Thoreau? 'The mass of men leading lives of quiet desperation?' That's the whole group of people who, whenever they are dwelling alone or amongst themselves, and conjuring a situation — a fact of life — who won a football game and why not, they always are thinking and talking in terms of the way that things ought to be. That is irony. 'I'd have done this,' or 'I think he should have done this,' so they are dealing not in reality but the way they think things ought to be. Things aren't always the way they should be, but they are always the way they are. Aristotle said it best: 'What is, is.'

"So you've got the Tom Dooleys of this world who see things the way they really are and try to change them to make them the way they should be. That's Tom Dooley or Albert Schweitzer. Then you've got this mass of people who see things the way they'd like them to be and dwell on it. Then you've got a few people who see things the way they really are, just like Albert, but deal with it that way to their advantage. They don't take that step of trying to change reality. Rather, they simply deal with reality.

"So when I look at my goal or a deal or whatever, I am looking at the reality of it. It prevents me from kidding myself and therefore I say: I have no path to the goal. It breaks down my goal attainment process. So I say NO. Emphatically, and forever and ever. No. And I'm gonna keep saying no if there is no way to wire the deal. I refuse to be romanced."

The next holes, which are amazing in their beauty and difficulty, went by in a blur. It is the same feeling I have after driving down a highway deep in thought only to realize that I don't remember any of the miles that have just flown by. Was I in control of the vehicle? Could I have avoided danger had it presented itself? Truly on auto-pilot.

We spent those last three holes reviewing the formula for goal attainment and reviewing what I now call the paradox of risk.

I think we went over the formula two or three times to implant it in my brain, which was only then becoming accustomed to these kinds of concepts. Remember, up until this epiphany, my *raison d'etre* had been golf, girls, hanging out, the usual pursuits of a 20-year-old.

I later wrote it down in my diary:

Step One: Define Your Goal

You ain't got one until you can say it and visualize it and feel it.

Step Two: Smell Test

Is your goal right? Is the goal morally and ethically right to do?

Step Three: See the Path

Make sure that you know the way to reach your goal. This is your plan, your strategy. Here you must be hyper-realistic. If you can't see the path, then you only have a dream. Don't start unless you can see the path to the goal.

Step Four: Commit

Commitment is truly the difference between success and failure. Do not bluff: Bet the pot that you will reach your goal. No one can defeat you if they see you are willing to give your all to win.

Step Five: Pass Go

Start. Go. Just do it. Graduate from beer talk.

The corollary to goal attainment is the **paradox of risk.** This is the Rosetta Stone of success. And it is this: If you personally can't wire the deal, don't go.

When Bob revealed that to me, I had no idea how profound the concept was. During the past 20 or so years, I have observed the success of entrepreneurs or business people and marveled at their tolerance for risk. But as I studied and looked more closely at their successes, and after interviewing many successful entrepreneurs, it was apparent that when they had succeeded it was because the deal had been wired, sometimes by accident.

His admonition to stay grounded in reality and to say NO when the path was not there prevented me from so many wrong turns. And when I have made mistakes, invariably I had unresolved path problems.

As we strolled up the 18th fairway, Bob fired one more brain-seeking missile my direction, "Scotty, let me give you one more contrarian piece of advice. Share."

"Share?"

"Yep. I call it the **abundancy theory** and it has worked beautifully for me. This is totally contrarian. In a world where knowledge is power, the conventional thing to do is to hoard what you know in a miserly fashion. You know how this works. If I know something that you don't know, I'm smarter, right? Wrong. I never figured it that way and it has paid off for me so many more times over than if I had kept what I knew to myself. The more you share, the more you learn. Most people really would like to share but they are afraid to. If you develop people's trust by being forthright, they will tell you their inner-most secrets.

"In business, this sharing of information has been a marvelous tool for us. By being open we have built trust with our employees and our customers. It has brought us many, many deals because people know what we are all about and what we are looking for. There is also something about sharing that is just the right thing to do. It feels good to do it. So as a company, we have always given away what our competition tries to charge for. Information, good information, is the value-added competitive edge that we offer our clientele. You can't compete with it. We kill our competition because of it. I can't tell you how important that part of our philosophy has been to our success. So do yourself a big favor, Scotty, share."

As we finished the last hole (Bob parred it for a 79), I began searching for a way to thank Bob for allowing me into his private classroom of life. Suddenly, it occurred to me! I knew I could appeal to his contrarian nature by doing to him what he had done to me. Yep. I stiffed him. As hard as he tried, I just wouldn't take his $50 bill. Finally, I had to tell him, "Bob, please. Even if you don't believe it, do me the honor of treating me with the respect I want to deserve. What you laid on me today was so incredibly valuable, it makes a few bucks trivial." (I spewed that out with conviction, although $50 was a big number to me then.)

He smiled, shrugged his shoulders, stuck it in his pocket and said, "Scotty, me boy, I'll bet it for you in Vegas."

The first major lesson on goal attainment had been a miracle. It was like giving sight to the blind. That morning I had been a wretched, uncoachable lad with the consciousness of a tee marker; later I felt enlightenment. O'Brien had etched upon my brain in such vividness, a map. And that map was going to lead me wherever I needed or wanted to go. I felt like Indiana Jones. I wasn't sure why that lesson stuck when so many others had failed to do so. I now think it made such a huge impression because Bob had gifted me when he had no reason to do so. I had certainly not given him just cause. But he was obviously a successful man, who had seen in me some glimmer of redemption, who through his generosity had opened a door in me that I hadn't known existed.

The five steps of goal attainment became my mantra. I saw its application everywhere I turned. And soon it became clear to me that not only did it work, but that I possessed a methodology that no one else seemed to have. I was seeing the world in full technicolor while everyone else was in black and white. That summer I became like a desert nomad thirsting for additional metaphors for my dehydrated brain. And I adopted the O'Brien method of contrarianism. Whenever a good lesson was imparted by gurus whose bags I carried, I stiffed them. It didn't happen that many times that summer, but that wasn't for lack of effort on my part or Richard's. Rich became my mentor lookout, always trying to hook me up with a potential teacher. I would loop for O'Brien four more times. Fortunately, there were several other "masters" who graced the National links that summer and their lessons became a part of my diary.

DISTANCE to the GREEN

JUNE 7

Mirror Phenomenon

The seventh is my birthday, although after 20 years my wife still thinks it's the sixth. My birthday has always been a lucky day for me, and something told me that this one was going to continue the trend. The previous two days had netted me about $130 in tips. I had not "stiffed" anyone since O'Brien, although I had tried to engage all my potential tutors in philosophical discussions. One industrialist had finally said to me, "Shut up, kid, and give me my wedge."

But the dawn of the seventh broke beautifully. Looking out from the caddyshack each morning we could watch the sun magically illuminate the dew and steam rise from the lakes. The patina cast by the dew was broken only by the tires of the mowers tracking their way to the greens. And once the greens were mowed, the verdant hue of the putting surface was startling. The tranquillity of the morning was broken by those same mowers humming away in the distance. A kind of industrial cicada courtesy of John Deere. The seventh felt good.

I loved being with first group off, the "dew sweepers." And that morning, Rich had assigned me to carry the bag of one Jorgen Jensen, a Danish shipping mogul. Jorgen — pronounced "Yorgen" — was not really a golfer. He was a tennis player, but being the gentleman he truly was, he had agreed to play with a group of American businessmen. His company was entertaining them in hopes of landing a huge contract to ship those products you see advertised on television, the *Veg-o-matic*, *Ginshu* knives, *Pocket Fisherman*, *Bass-o-Matic*, individually wrapped links of dental floss, really weird stuff that the rational mind should reject but that always seems to appeal to the American consumer. Jorgen was quite amused by the cargo. His Scandinavian perspective rejected this frivolous materialism, but he was very happy to convey the tons of crap that these fellows were ready to shill.

That morning Jorgen gave me three important lessons, and I looked forward to stiffing him. Perhaps the biggest lesson he left with me was his uncommon civility and courtliness. I had never been exposed to Europeans, so I assumed they might all be like Jorgen. I have learned since that he was remarkable in many respects. He spoke seven languages including Japanese. But he possessed a calm that was remarkable and a respect for humanity that came from down deep. His gentle wisdom was so profound that I remember it even today. A thousand times since I have thought that if everyone possessed this embodiment of the golden rule, what a wonderful place the world would be.

I pondered for the longest time what gave Jorgen a sort of magnetism. I noticed that day that people wanted to visit with Jorgen, they wanted his attention, they brightened up when he spoke to them. I know I was unable to articulate it at the time, but I came to believe his special gift was the fact that he radiated his belief in the basic goodness of people. And many years later, I miraculously and literally bumped into Jorgen in Maui at the summit of the Haleakala Crater and had the opportunity to talk to him about this. He told me that he thought that his philosophy was centered around the idea of trust.

Trust, he told me, was what gave him his wonderful outlook on things. He explained its valuable power to open others to dialogue.

He told marvelous stories of how trust had allowed his company to function as a team and that jealousies and petty politics were just not possible in an environment of trust. He related the intensity and closeness of relationships that he had built on trust. When I asked him about experiences of trust betrayed, he shrugged and said that happened from time to time, but the cost of abandoning his philosophy was tremendously more expensive than to continue forward believing in the goodness of people. He said I would be surprised at how many people would respond to trust because they found it so refreshing and liberating.

His bag was very light that day as he imparted two lessons that became part of that summer's education. The first was a simple little story that reconfirmed what O'Brien had schooled me on only a few days before. It was related to the smell test in goal attainment but with a slightly different metaphor.

Jorgen told me a story of his mentor, the head of the largest shipping line in the world. He told me that he had heard this gentleman quietly — but with deadly precision — deflate the rationalization of one of Jorgen's peers. The young man had a task that had required all of his talents, and the young man had gone to great lengths to achieve his goal. Using all his intellect and guile, he had nonetheless fallen short and knew it. He came to the old master and dutifully reported his near-miss, explaining that he had done this, tried that, and regaled the old man with his tale of tribulation. After completing his woeful story, he slumped back in his chair content that his boss knew he had given his best efforts. A rueful smile crept across the old man's face, then suddenly his eyes grew stormy. "First," he said, "I have little use for excuses. We built (and he did say 'we') this company into the world's largest by each of us taking responsibility. And I can see that lesson hasn't eluded you. I commend you for your ability to deliver this disappointing news. And I can see that you have done 'your best.' But you have not succeeded and the reason that you have not succeeded is that although you gave your best, you did not do the right thing: the right thing." And with that the old man looked down at his reports signaling the end of the conversation.

Here I was, nearly at the end of my college career, and in the space of a few days I had learned more about how to get to where I wanted to go than I had in all the time leading up to my sentence to National. In fact, these moments of enlightenment were coming with such regularity that I believed they had been there all the time for the taking if I had just been aware or ready.

The message Jorgen's master had taught him was so obvious. Why hadn't I been able to see something so plain? "Don't just do your best. You must do the right thing." I must stop my life as a human nerf ball, bouncing from one thing to another without enough mass to do myself or others any harm, and I must set about to do the RIGHT thing. More than ever, O'Brien's lesson about goal attainment was the perfect tool for me to achieve whatever was required. Bob had talked about defining the goal, submitting it to the smell test (was it right?) and then seeing the path followed by committing one's full efforts (not just best efforts.) Then doing it unreservedly. It was the exact formula that Jorgen's master had laid out so succinctly when he told his chagrined protégé that it wasn't enough just to do your best, that he had to do the right thing as well. They were the same. Bob had given me a map for my future. Jorgen had confirmed it.

Then he let me in on one of the most valuable secrets I'd ever be privy to. We were walking up a slope to the tee of the 6th, from whose height you can look back over portions of the course you have just traversed.

"Have you ever wanted to be someone you're not?" Jorgen

46

asked me. "I don't mean wanting to be a movie star or desiring all sorts of material wealth. I'm talking about wanting to be one of those rare people who can walk into a room and the atmosphere changes."

"Sure," I said. I thought about O'Brien and how he was one of those guys who just by looking at him you knew he commanded your respect. I wanted to be just like that, not just the money — although that part would be nice — but I wanted to have that kind of aura, where people knew immediately that you weren't some doormat. You were a force to be reckoned with. Looping for people like that and trodding along with their bags had made me know exactly what Jorgen meant.

He was silent as he set up for his tee off, allowing me to reflect on the kind of people I admired. He awkwardly whacked in the general direction of the green with a shot that put him in the tree line to the right of where he should have been.

"There's something I learned as a boy in a private school in Switzerland. It's going to sound a bit juvenile in some way perhaps, but I guarantee it is not — nor are the results," Jorgen offered as we headed toward his ball. "Today, I call it the **mirror phenomenon** and it works beautifully if you're willing to make the effort."

"The mirror phenomenon?" I laughed. "Don't tell me this is where I stand in front of a mirror each morning telling myself how intelligent and handsome I am."

He smiled in his wry way.

"No, that is probably an American secret to superpower," Jorgen said. "This is mine. There is a formula to become the kind of person you want to be. The premise is that if, say, you are a B or a C or a D — something other than an A, and you want to be an A —this is the formula to become an A. It's very simple and it works."

He took a moment to shove his ball off again, overcompensating a bit for his earlier off-kilter drive. I really hoped at that moment that Jorgen was a good tennis player because his golf game was rudimentary. The more he talked, the more strokes he took to get on the green, but I wasn't minding.

"If you're a B and you want to be an A, the first thing you do is you study what an A looks like. How does an A behave? How does an A dress? How does an A deport herself or himself? You start to get an image and pretty soon you own the essence of an A."

I nodded. So far this was stuff I was starting to do subconsciously anyway.

"You're a B, but you dissect an A," Jorgen continued. "That's step one. Step two, you start acting like an A — just like you're on stage. You emulate an A. You start behaving like an A, start dressing like an A, start talking like an A. For all intents and purposes, you're an A. Now the next thing that happens is that people notice. You see, most people want to put others in a box."

"A box?" I asked. Up to that point, I was somewhat naive about the base aspects of human nature and how to use them to my advantage.

"Well, they want to label you. You are a — how do you say it here? — a nerd?"

"Right," I laughed. "You're a nerd, or a football player or a cheerleader."

"Yes," he said. "Or you're an A and that's okay, too. They don't care what you are. They just want to know. They want to put you in an A box or a B box or a C box. They just want to get you characterized. They don't want to take a B and make him into an A — no one has time to do that. If you're a nerd, they put you in the nerd box. If you're a cheerleader, they put you in the cheerleader box. If you're an all-star quarterback, they put you in the all-star quarterback box. People do not care, so long as they know what box you're in and you stay in your box."

Finally, we were on the green and I handed Jorgen his putter for the four-foot downhill putt he needed to finish off this hole with a double bogey. He focused an extra minute and sunk it.

"So, the third thing that happens — particularly to people who've never known you before but even to those who have — you are looking like an A, you're acting like an A. As far as they're concerned, what are you?"

"You're an A," I replied.

"You are an A," Jorgen confirmed. "Certainly, they are going to put you in the A box. They're not going to put you in a B box or a C box or a D box or an E box. They will put you in the A box. If they've already known you, they're confused for a while, but because they don't really care, they will pull you out of your old box and put you in the A box. You've become an A. Theirs is not to wonder why, but to put you in the A box.

"Now, that's step three. You're in their A box. Step four takes place. They start and when they deal with you, how do they deal with you?"

"As if you're an A," I answered again.

"Yes! You're in the A box so they deal with you like an A. They are sending you 'You're an A' signals or they are sending you 'You're a nerd signals' or they are sending you 'You're a B' signals. Therefore, it follows that if you are sending A signals and you're getting back A signals, what are you? You are an A. What else are you? We're not talking rocket science here, we are talking social style. Social interaction. We're not talking about what's going on in your head. We're talking about your relationships with other people. You could be a scumbag or con artist, but on a social interpersonal basis, for all practical purposes, you are a Methodist minister.

49

"So, the mirror phenomenon is that you can become an A," Jorgen said as I shouldered his bag again for the walk. "The applications of that are so magnificent that you can learn to be various things as the occasion demands. If you want to be a 'Dom Perignon, anyone?' kind of fellow, you can as long as you know what to do. Then you can go down to the watering hole and tap the keg with your 'tough bar rat' persona."

"But isn't that just acting and getting people to believe you? It's not real," I said.

"Oh, Scotty, but it is real," Jorgen replied. "You have studied what it takes to become an A. You do those things — you metamorphosize — and it just follows that people follow. Think about those people you said you admired. Are they acting or is it real? It doesn't matter as long as you are treating them as an A, for example. The only thing you must remember: Don't abuse this tool. If you are a phony, trust ceases."

I knew he was right. If other people could do that, so could I. I knew several days ago that I wanted to be an A — a Bob O'Brien kind of guy. And thanks to the forethought of Rich Nelson, I was to have several other people to study as well.

I don't know how Jorgen knew of my thirst for this wisdom or enlightenment. Just as with Bob O'Brien, I was flattered that Jorgen had seen me worthy of his mentorship. I was starting to develop several theories about their generosity. One common denominator was Bob's admonition to share the knowledge. When a person has "made" it and he really knows who he is, the wisdom that allowed him to achieve is not squirreled away in a miserly fashion. Bob's abundancy theory is shared by those who appreciate that they are constant learners as well as teachers.

Secondly, people like Bob and Jorgen do not fear the intimacy that is a part of sharing and opening up. In fact, it is just the opposite. They relish the opportunity to explore the inner workings of their fellow travelers along the journey. Though I sensed this tendency toward openness, I also suspected these men were not prone to empty blathering and saved their good stuff for those for whom it would do the most good. They saw something redemptive in me — and I was the very fortunate and appreciative recipient of their mentoring.

My birthday had been another lucky day. The gifts bestowed upon me that day remain with me even now. Nothing material could have meant as much. Jorgen, of course, tried to reward the physical efforts of my caddying, but I was thrilled to be able to stiff him as I had O'Brien.

Like Bob, Jorgen thought my barter system of knowledge in lieu of cash was really refreshing, and I was pleased that he understood. It left the ledger balanced as I entered my 22nd year.

Hell, come fall, Coach Robbie was liable to call up trying find out who they sent back in my body.

DISTANCE TO THE GREEN

JUNE 11

Comrades in Arms: George and NuWay

The four days leading up to June 11 were uneventful. I was fortunate to carry for two golfers each day. My cash position was improving, but my storehouse of knowledge had not increased. The golfers I had looped for were the typical National members: well-mannered, generally nice people, affluent, but mostly interested in the concerns of the other members of their group. Sometimes there was friendly wagering, sometimes not-so-friendly. Most members of National are very, very successful in their field. They are also very competitive. The intensity of the competition is a wonderment to behold when two or more high rollers square off. It was not rare during golf matches that summer that $1,000 would change hands.

The typical high stakes game was a "Nassau." Usually the Nassau was $100 or more per side. The player or team that is behind can start a new bet, so by the end of the side, there may be four, five or more bets going. Strategic betting, factoring in the handicaps of all the players, is important in coming out ahead. Golf has dozens of betting games that make the round "interesting."

June 11 was significant because of the addition of a new caddie. George Spachmann joined our crew that day. It was apparent almost immediately that George was not like the other members of the caddie family at National. Back in those days we had an expression that is still used for guys like George. He was a "stud."

Now that terminology was not indicative of anything having to do with sex, although given George's athletic build and good looks, I'm sure he was very successful in that regard. "Stud" to us was a convenient way for us to begrudgingly admit our admiration for his appearance and, more importantly, his aura. George had a bravura like Paul Newman in the movie *Cool Hand Luke*. He was confident, not cocky. He always seemed to have the right offhand comment that was just perfect for the moment — and he had it quickly. I'll bet George never walked away from a conversation thinking, "Gee, I wish I had said so-and-so."

There was no way *not* to like George. If you remember high school days, you will recall that in every school there were four or five guys who set the tone for everyone else. The way they dressed was the coolest. What they chose to do was what we all wanted to do. And if they deemed you one of their group, you were made. You were somebody. If George suggested that we go out to get a cheeseburger, then we went with the full knowledge that it was THE place to be at that moment in that part of the universe.

Another remarkable thing about George was that he was deep. He was a remarkable blend of brains, street smarts and looks. I have met a lot of people over the years, but few had the package George had.

George and I took an immediate liking to one another. On his first day at National, Rich wisely paired us up. I guess we thought of ourselves as being quite a bit different from the other guys who called the caddyshack home that summer. Part of my education that summer included the time George and I spent together bouncing our ideas and theories off one another. The simpatico of that relationship with George allowed me to sound out my new-found lessons and by verbalizing them, they became more crystalline and fixed in my mind.

Comrades in Arms: George and NuWay

George's and my routine consisted of our daily loops followed by dinner with the other guys and then we headed off to NuWay. NuWay was a drive-in in the classic sense. It was straight out of *American Graffiti*, car hops outside and faded orange Naugahyde booths on the inside. And the booth in the corner was ours. We spent hours there that summer covering every topic.

Interestingly, George also held my new-found theory (from Bob O'Brien) that sharing knowledge was the way to go. We became convinced that if he knew what I knew and I knew what he knew, we were both better off. It was win-win. That sharing of knowledge was one of O'Brien's cornerstones of success, and it became George's and mine. We knew if we did that, we would know more than anybody else, because all they knew was what they knew themselves. We knew we would be smarter than they were in terms of reasoning — not necessarily IQ— but reasoning, wisdom. That's different and more important than pure IQ.

We became philosophers that summer. We were into heavy thinking. It was a wonderful form of entertainment, competition, adrenaline-producing intellectual stimulation — it offered everything.

June 11 marked the beginning of a marvelous partnership between us. I can still remember the first enlightened moment that we shared. Because we were both in college at the time, one of our initial topics of discussion was our academic misadventures. My grades had been fine, although I was an under-achiever of sorts. Until that point I had not truly distinguished between really learning something and making a grade. So my study habits tended to be slipshod, and I relied heavily on my above-average, short-term memory to get by.

George had a different slant on learning which he shared with me that first night at the NuWay. He told me a story about his high school algebra teacher, Dr. Lasley. Seems George's older sister was an academic wiz at their high school. His sister, and mine for that matter, were the type of students who made a Dr. Lasley willing and proud to be a teacher. Real students. So he got another Spachmann in there and he thought he had another real student. Well, George was struggling with algebra, really struggling. So Dr. Lasley asked him to come in after school. George went and talked to Dr. Lasley and in about an hour he turned him from a dunce in philosophy — philosophy, not algebra — into a philosopher.

George told me, "In an hour, he unbound me in the sense of what was going on in my mind. For example, I was taking algebra, the subject of algebra, and I was trying to work each problem as if it were unique. I thought I had to memorize something to get it. The fact was that the numbers were just a way of reducing it to something portable, transferable. Dr. Lasley told me, 'The numbers don't make any difference. You are never going to have to know this formula. What's this formula mean? What is it's value? It has no value. But the solving of the formula is everything. It is a process, a way of thinking. So we simply reduce it to numbers to give you a basis to learn.'

"And this is what he said that had so much meaning. He said the number of algebraic equations is infinite. If you try to solve them in any way other than an infinite way, you're lost. You're going to try to memorize an infinite number of solutions to equations? Absurd! So he taught me how to do it, and it taught me how to diagram sentences, how to conjugate verbs, how to read classics. All because it was a way of thinking."

When George got to that point of his story, I was hit by another blinding flash of light. I guess that was the summer of cognition, because these flashes of light were coming regularly. Dr. Lasley's method of solving problems seemed to affirm step three of

O'Brien's goal attainment formula. Step three is "see the path," all about getting the correct thought process. On June 11, the tumblers were starting to click into place.

DISTANCE TO THE GREEN

JUNE 17

Control = Happiness

As I mentioned, I caddied with Bob O'Brien more than I caddied for anyone else, but I had several "mentors" in addition to Bob as the summer progressed. Each provided a perspective that I could not have gotten anywhere except on that sacred golf ground at National. Perhaps the most idiosyncratic fellow I caddied for that summer was part of an afternoon foursome on June 17. My diary from that day is filled with exclamation marks. I had come to appreciate O'Brien's brand of contrarianism, but Christopher Schnebley Case was truly one of a kind. He was especially unique given the time and place. For a guy like C.S. Case to find himself in any foursome at National had to have been some sort of mistake.

C.S. is one of, if not the wackiest person to ever address the dimpled orb at National. To say he was a man ahead of his time was a gross understatement. Case was a brilliantly successful entrepreneur. He could spot a trend or create a trend like no other. He prided himself on his ability to look at a problem or situation from a totally different angle. On June 17, I initially mistook him for some sort of reprobate who by some error had snuck through National's security system and now had access to the course. But the fact that Rich had assigned me to carry his bag (his own invention to which he had added pop-out legs so the bag stood by itself — predating the popular bag of the '90s by some 15 years) affirmed his legitimacy.

His appearance was really odd for his time. He sported long hair (not unusual except at National), which he wore in a pony tail, and a goatee. He wore sneakers with dozens of little nubs on the bottom instead of golf shoes, and he dressed all in black, a la Gary Player.

His swing and putting stroke were equally queer. He literally stepped into the ball, cocking his left leg like a home-run hitter, lifting his left toe about six inches above the ground, then sliding forward about six inches. The effect was a total 100 percent transference of his weight from the back leg to the front (which is very sound). His left arm, though rigid and straight at impact, was awkwardly bent at the top of his swing. His distance for a relatively small man was prodigious. He had a closed stance and played a nice draw on every shot. He used a cross-handed split grip on his putting stroke and made everything. The notes in my diary show that he shot 76 that day and there was some serious wagering going on. After all, who wouldn't have wanted a piece of C.S. Case after seeing his swing?

The details of his game are worthy of inclusion in this retelling of my summer just for the sheer delight of recalling that odd swing and the monetary result. Frankly, I had previously caddied for a couple of the guys he wore out that day, and they were ripe for it. The two I knew were especially cocky both on and off the course. Most of the players at National are super people. They are wealthy and successful, and for the most part, they are gracious and cordial. I'm sure as much of their success is due to their ability to handle relationships as it is their brain wattage.

Christopher Schnebley Case's story, if it was all true, was really remarkable. Schnebley is an old family name dating back to his great-great-great grandfather, who was one of the original white settlers of Sedona, Arizona. Now if you know anything about

Sedona you know that many of its citizens hear the beat of a different cosmic drummer. I believe that Sedona must be Exalted World Headquarters for the "New Age." You know — Shirley McLaine, crystals, channeling, pyramid power, et al. In fact, the Sedona area is home to something like seven vortices. A vortex is a place where all sorts of mystical power, both negative and positive, emanate from the earth. The Native Americans first identified these sacred grounds, but it took the white man to commercialize the swirling enchantment of Mother Earth. Let's just say that C.S. Case was a chip off the old crystal of grandpappy.

Despite his otherworldliness, C.S. was full of lessons. And I was going to stiff him, but he was so weird I didn't think he was going to tip me anyway. But I am getting ahead of myself.

The first C.S. lesson was obvious: You can't judge a book by its cover. Despite his outward iconoclastic behavior, he had thought every concept through. Just like O'Brien, he "knew the path." He undoubtedly knew his goal, knew the path, and made a commitment. During the round he rarely spoke to his playing partners but was really talkative to me. Maybe he sensed my openness to new ideas or just didn't feel like talking to the other three. I already mentioned my antipathy for them, so perhaps he was just a good judge of character.

Anyway, it was my good fortune to discover a great deal about Mr. Case. Turned out Case was, like most of the players at National, very wealthy. He had made his fortune importing or manufacturing the latest wave of hot products. He had made a killing as an early seller of waterbeds. Over the years he had a string of successes by being one step ahead of the pack: VCRs, computers and software, airbags, and his latest was a resin that was 10 times stronger than concrete, wouldn't burn to 2,000 degrees and floated.

Case wore this really unusual leather braid necklace that had a crystal of some sort woven into it as a pendant. He noticed me studying it.

"David," he called me by my given name, which was one of the few times during the summer that I wasn't referred to by my nickname, "this pendant holds mysterious and wondrous properties. I never go out without it, and I don't dare test the fates to do otherwise. The crystal was given to me by an old woman who lived up in Oak Creek Canyon north of Sedona. She was generally considered a hermit by all and a witch by some. Her psychic powers were legendary. On two occasions she was credited with locating children who had gotten lost in the canyons. She had sort of a gypsy's evil eye and if she cast it over you, it sent a chill clean down to your toes. But if her scrutiny revealed a pure spirit and character, you could count on her powers to be allied with yours.

I met her in my 10th summer. I was hiking and exploring up around 7,500 feet when I came across a young cougar cub. Cute as hell, so knowing no better I picked her up. David, do you have any idea how protective a mother cougar is?" he laughed. "Well, I was just about to find out. From over the ridge, maybe 60 yards away, came Mama and she was flying. You can't believe the speed of a big cat on a maternal rescue mission. I dropped the cub and started to run for a rock, a tree, anything to lose Mama Cougar.

"So I was running as fast as I could, looking over my shoulder, watching this beast close that 60 yards incredibly fast. Out from behind a boulder stepped this little old lady dressed in loose-fitting gray robes. Softly she said, 'Get behind me.'

"She stood perfectly still as the cat continued its incredible pace towards us. When the cat was about 20 feet away, the old lady stretched out her arm and opened up her hand so that the cat could see what she was holding in her palm. It was a collection of what appeared to be shiny, multi-colored stones. The cat stopped. She lowered her head and I heard the most incredible sound I have ever heard before or since. The Mama cougar started to purr. Now if you've ever heard a house cat purr, it can be pretty loud sometimes. This cat was eight times bigger and this purring was really something. With head bowed, Mama headed back to baby cougar.

"The old lady turned around, knelt down and looked me right in the eyes. Of course, I was shaking like a leaf, trying not to cry, happy to be among the living, and scared out of my mind that I'd gone from jaws of the mountain lion into the coven of the mountain witch.

"I felt the chill of her gaze, but her voice was warm, 'Little one, take this crystal. Keep it with you always. It will protect you from those who would steal your purity.' And then she moved silently back into the forest of lodgepole pines.

She was a legend in those parts. I would see her from time to time down in Sedona, especially at the psychic, new age events. Anyway, I've kept this crystal with me for over 30 years."

"What about the necklace? I have never seen anything like that."

"David, that is a beautiful story, too. A Navajo chief gave it to me in 1952. My girlfriend and I set out on a cross-country adventure that summer and we decided to spend some time up in the Four Corners area on the Navajo Reservation. Hitchhiking is very popular on the reservation. We picked up a man. Turned out he was a chief on the reservation. His name was Harry Coolwater. Harry thanked us for the ride in two ways as we transported him to Window Rock. First, he noticed the crystal which I had hung from the mirror of my '49 Chevy pickup on a loop of hemp, which could also serve as a sort of necklace. Harry was a master leather craftsman and in his pouch he had several lengths of buffalo hide. It was astonishing to watch his fingers magically weave a type of sling for the crystal and then braid a necklace that has stayed in one piece to this day. It has only become more beautiful as my body oils and the weather have tanned it to perfection.

"While he wove this piece, he spoke about his life on the reservation and some of his beliefs. Of course, we had never heard such philosophy, but much like you, David, if my guess is right, we were seekers after knowledge. That was in fact our mission. Well, most of it," he grinned. "My girlfriend and I had an incredibly passionate, physical relationship that we could never seem to satisfy.

"Harry repaid my ride that day with a bit of Navajo philosophy that has helped guide me throughout my life. He called it 'The Way.' I call it living in harmony. The Navajos seek to balance their lives. They know if something gets out of whack, there will be a counter-balancing force to pull things back into order. It's a metaphysical force that is stronger than we are and to fight it is foolish, so the best approach is to accept it and get with its program. For instance, the Navajo live in the high desert. Not much rain there, so they have to harmonize their existence with the conditions. During a drought, the other tribes might do a rain dance or a white man might resort to cloud seeding, but the Navajos adapt to the conditions.

"As I have moved through life, I have seen over and over the foolish attempts of people to try to change those things they couldn't or to rail against the perceived injustices of life when their path should have been to seek harmony. The concept of balance has been a profound guiding principle for me. Keeping things in perspective. Knowing what the really important things in life are.

"Let me give you another example. How many times have you heard members come to this beautiful place and spend their time here complaining? Complaining about business, complaining about pressures, complaining that they don't have enough time, complaining about their wives and/or their girlfriends. It's absurd. These people have more gifts and opportunities than most and not an ounce of appreciation. And definitely no harmony or balance. Have no clue what they have.

"I love it when I hear them complain about the pressures of their lives. There are good pressures and bad pressures. You can see the toll of the bad pressures. If you have money problems, health problems, family problems, moral or ethical problems, you will wear them like scars. The price is huge. I think the Bible calls them the 'wages of sin.'

"But there are good pressures, too. The pressure to excel and compete and create makes you alive and vibrant. There is nothing so exhilarating as setting a goal and achieving it. Just make sure you take a moment to savor what you have accomplished.

"Look, David, we are all blessed with one commodity — our time. Invest it, don't waste it on efforts that will poison your spirit. That was what Chief Harry taught me that day. Out-of-harmony thoughts and deeds are toxins. They poison our lives. The real evil of 'corporate American life' is that at the end of the day, if you are not careful it will steal from your most precious possession: your time. I see guys working 70 or 80 hours a week. Totally out of harmony, high blood pressure, heart palpitations, always tired, thinking that the money they are earning can buy back the time they are missing from their families. Hard work and its rewards are marvelous, fantastic, but not when there isn't balance in your life."

Case was amazing. Here was this man who looked to be the odd duck among this foursome of business people, and I guess he was, but he was the man with the most traditional and sound values. I vowed then to seek a harmonious path and a singular, solitary path if necessary.

Our discussion of harmony took us to the turn at National. Case finished the first 9 holes in 2 over par — 38. His high-powered, short-haired, Sansabelted playing partners were scowling. Although they weren't saying it, they were mentally computing the fact that they had lost about $300 on the front 9 to this odd little guy with the weird swing. When they stepped up on the 10th tee, the cockiest of the bunch, Don (short for Donovan) Ashworth, let his ego get the best of him. And like many a risk taker who doesn't have his deal wired, he doubled the bet. At first C.S. hesitated, but sensing that Ashworth certainly wasn't in harmony, he decided to accept Don's offer. Other fools decided to rush in, so C.S. had three pigeons to fleece on the back 9. Despite what would have been enormous pressure on an impoverished college student like me, Case had plenty of money, so the game to him was one of skill and concentration. He refused to let his ego become involved and that was his most deadly weapon in match play. He could be beaten by a hot player, but he refused to beat himself.

So off we went. For Mr. Case and me, the pace, the temperament and the conversation were unchanged. For Donovan Ashworth and his buddies, it was going to be an excruciating two hours of anxiety and frustration. They were whipped before they teed it up on Number 10.

Case's swing on his drive on 10 was his usual unorthodox effort, but I started to see the beauty in its efficiency and, actually, it was silky smooth. The back 9 was about to become a great lesson in control. Case personified it and he was also kind enough to talk about it as he went about separating the fools from their money.

"David, if my guess is right and I play my usual game, these boys will tie themselves in knots before the afternoon is over. First, they aren't as good as they would like to think they are. Secondly, they think my game is a fluke. Lastly, with this much money at stake they are going to press. That will really screw up any chance they might have. You watch. Their wheels will start to come off as soon as the rub of the green goes against them. I won't have to shoot 40 to whip these boys."

And, of course, he was right. The back 9 at National is no place to blow your cool. It will flat eat your lunch if you don't manage the course and play patiently. By course management, I mean you have to play your shots so each one sets up the next one. Like an expert billiards player. Each shot is two shots: the shot at hand and the next one.

National's fairways are shaped so that reaching the green is often first a matter of directing your tee shot to the proper side of the fairway. And the greens are so tricky that your approach shot to the green must be positioned so that the dreaded three or four putt isn't likely. Due to the slope of most of the greens, if you are above the hole, I guarantee you, gravity will not be friendly. It is common for those types of putts to roll completely off the front of the green. The severe slope of several of the tiered greens bedevil even the expert putters, with putts failing to climb the slope and the putter watching his ball not only return to him but come to rest further from the hole. These factors were precisely what Case was talking about when he spoke of control and patience. National will give up some birdies to the patient golfer, but it will severely penalize the imprudent golfer who lets his ego get the best of him.

And Donovan had a huge ego. Trying to match Case's well-placed and long tee ball, he swung extra hard, destroying his tempo and pushing his tee ball over to a tree line that frames the right side of the fairway. Finding himself slightly blocked from the green by a 150-year-old oak tree, he opted to try to hit a miracle fade towards the green. Swinging even harder than on his tee shot, he hit his second shot through the fairway, into a grove of trees on the other side of the fairway. It just so happened that my buddy George was caddying for Donovan. I caught George's exasperation because I know he had advised him to just punch the ball out in the fairway and hope to get the third shot close. I also knew that George was hoping Case would take the wind out of this blowhard's sails, even if it meant Ashworth's cash would be depleted, as would George's tip.

Ashworth's third shot was another attempt at a miracle. He was able to thread his punched 4-iron through the trees and right into the deepest bunker guarding the green. Of course, my guy has 155 to the green after his drive and he hits an easy 6-iron to the middle of the green. Ashworth hits a pretty good sand shot to about 10 feet from the hole. But the wrong side of the hole. He has a downhill, left to right breaking putt. He was very, very lucky to 2 putt for his double bogey. C.S. lags his 20-footer to a spot about one foot below the cup and taps in for par. Before they even get off the green, Ashworth says, "You're X'd, Case." X'd meant that he was redoubling the bet! Case winked at me, a sly smile creasing his tanned face.

"David, this is a perfectly example of an equation that I formed years ago and has yet to be contradicted in all my experience... control = happiness. No, I take that back, roller coaster rides are the one exception. Seriously, David, the person in control has the upper hand in all things. Let's think about why my equation is so true. If our personal lives are out of control, we are anxious and not happy. If our personal relationships, our friendships, romances, marriages are out of control, invariably we will be unhappy. If our emotions are out of control, if we are angry or nervous, we will never perform to our best or say the right things. When in control we can get in that zone that allows for peak performance. How do we feel if our financial life is out of control? We feel very anxious, and I guarantee you it will either dominate our thoughts or influence them subconsciously. Either way, we are unhappy. The feeling of well-being that a person has when things are in his control is sublimely magnificent.

Consider the man whose habits are not under his control. He may deceive himself into a belief that he is happy with himself but the truth is he is not happy to be a slave to his vices. Pity the man who is a slave to the bottle or cigarettes. A rich life is also unnatural. Live light, David, live light."

These sentiments were, of course, resonant. They were different ways of restating those important lessons from Bob and Jorgen and they were crystallizing in my heretofore empty head. The idea of control equaling happiness was really golden. The concept, like many others I had learned during that summer, was elegantly simple. On the surface it seemed straight-forward, basic and something that everyone should be aware of. But I realized that I hadn't thought in those terms and as I observed others around me, I realized they hadn't either.

These bromides were so universal that they quickly became guiding principles that could be relied on in any situation. Control = happiness was everywhere I looked. It sure was the case that afternoon as C.S. was taking Ashworth to the cleaners. The equation was working on two levels: Case was in control of his shots and Ashworth wasn't. Case was in control of his emotions and Ashworth wasn't. And if you were anywhere near the two men, you could immediately tell who was happy and who wasn't.

By the 15th hole, Ashworth was down to Case on four bets. While each man was putting, George and I would get off out of earshot, on the side of the green and discuss what was going on. I had filled George in on the control equation by the end of the 13th hole. After that, George was in on the game and was rooting for Case.

On 14, when Ashworth had a 7-footer to tie the hole, George muttered so only I could hear, "Miss it, Donovan, you over-grown, spoiled baby." Which he did and after which he promptly threw his putter about 50 feet. Yep, the wheels had definitely come off and Donovan was careening out of control. There was a major wreck awaiting on the 18th green.

By number 18, Donovan Ashworth was about to give up the game of golf. To add to his agony, Case birdied 18 while Donovan had one of his few pars on the back side. Donovan must carry a lot of cash, because he literally threw the $1,000 he'd lost at Case as he stomped off the course. After Ashworth had turned to walk back to the clubhouse, Case offered me $200. Now this was real temptation. That $200 would be my largest tip of the summer, but I had resolved very early in the round to "stiff" him, although as I had begun to appreciate him, I had changed my opinion about whether he would even offer a gratuity. Here was a true test of control = happiness. Could I control my greed — and would I be happy after I did so?

Well, it felt good to turn that money down. But I did so backhandedly. I suggested that Mr. Case give George something rather than me and I explained my policy of turning down quid pro quo lucre after someone had given me something worth more. Case got a big kick out this. He also figured that Ashworth wasn't likely to offer George anything (he didn't). "George, since this was Mr. Big Ticket's anyway, here's something for your trouble" and stuck a C-note in George's shirt pocket. Let me tell you, George and I had a great laugh and a BIG time that night and it wasn't at the NuWay. The next morning came very early and not without some pain.

JUNE 28

Problem Solving Through Creative Thinking

There was one hell of a thunderstorm yesterday. Most of the would-be swingers elected to stay in the clubhouse hitting Beefeater martinis and Glenlivet 18 rather than Titleists. With the course very wet and the weather still somewhat threatening, most of the competition would be at the gin rummy tables.

The grounds were still a bit damp when I joined the other caddies for breakfast before getting my next assignment from Richard. Some of the locals apparently had taken the weather as an opportunity to head to town and lose their week's tips to Goose on the pool table. The other guys endured his brutal ego all through breakfast while George and I ate quickly and awaited our fate in the outer lobby.

When Rich arrived, everyone else had joined us to get their looping assignments. I was to caddie for Diane Taylor Falona — not without comment from Goose ("Woman on the block!"). Everyone had heard about Diane. The other members at National referred to her with careful phrases like "free-spirited." Her husband, J. P. Falona, owned one the largest international advertising agencies in the world. Diane, according to the gossip circuit, had grown up on the south side of Chicago. She'd gotten into Georgetown's international policies program and commenced a career of becoming a "world citizen." She'd been a consultant to the State Department until she'd chosen the wrong side of the

Cuban Revolution. Despite her ousting, she had her own success-ful organization that provided press freedom and human rights information to the U.N. and other monitoring bodies. Rich said she and Falona met in Belfast about 15 years ago.

The clubhouse had been abuzz yesterday with word of her arrival. I wasn't sure what I was expecting, but it wasn't the five-foot brunette with a yellow sun hat who stuck her hand out to me.

"Hi, Scotty. Diane Falona," she said, and in one seamless move shook my hand and handed me her clubs.

"Nice to meet you. Are we waiting for anyone else?" I asked, not sure if she'd be with a foursome.

"No. Let's go," she said. She gave me a quizzical look as if to tell me I should have been briefed that she prefers to play alone.

The first three holes or so, she gave me the usual "getting to know you" quiz. By that time, I was pretty well prepared for all that. I was just hoping she wasn't going to quiz me on international cur-rent events. All I knew was what directly pertained to me, and the french fries at the NuWay were about the extent of that.

She had a peculiar way of talking to you. She'd stop whatever she was doing and study your face while you answered her ques-tions. You don't find people like that much anymore, especially in this crowd. Some of the people here ask you how you are and prob-ably would hardly notice if your hair were on fire. Diane was very intense and she hung on every word — even if you were a peon looper — as if the next one might be the secret passage to your soul.

I was kind of nervous because I had heard so much about her, and she wasted no time in finding out what I knew.

"Scotty, did you hear about my run in with the State Department several years ago?" Diane turned and faced me straight on. Well, as straight on as someone could who was a foot and a half shorter than I am.

Jeez, not only was I going to have to admit I'd heard the gossip, but then I'd have to confess I wouldn't know Castro from Mao Tse-Tung if I tripped over their cleats.

"Yes," I said, looking down, "someone was talking about that yesterday. That's too bad. I'm sorry."

She stood motionless for a second and then broke a smile.

"Don't be. Listen, I don't want to bore you with the details — they're irrelevant. I was sure you'd heard about it given the mouths here."

This time I gave her my now-perfected "no comment" grin. We strolled to the 6th hole, and my anxiety about committing some faux pas disappeared with the drifts of humid steam floating up from the drying course.

"Scotty, I hope you will learn earlier than I did that most people make decisions without all the facts. Few people have a system for making decisions and solving problems, which is why they tend to face the same ones over and over and never seem to get beyond where they are. If you can learn my method, it will help you in whatever you decide to do. It's actually very simple and its simplicity allows it to handle any level of complexity. I used this at the State Department to solve even the most complex foreign policy problems.

"For me, step one is to gather all of the facts about a problem, not just the ones I know or want to know. Gather all the facts: the good, the bad and the ugly. This means I've got to be liberated, freed up from all my prejudices, my personal biases, my involvement. I've got to get total perspective on the problem. I really see the short-comings of any other system when I'm gathered around a table trying to carve out a solution to a foreign policy problem and people have already chosen up sides. They want to advocate a solution before they know what the problem is. It drives me crazy.

"The way I do it is to lay all the pieces out so I know what I'm dealing with — like a jigsaw puzzle that's not framed in. Scotty, you've done jigsaw puzzles, haven't you? The first thing I work on is the border, defining the edges. I don't know yet whether I've got all of the pieces or whether I've got them in the right sequence.

"Sequence is very important, and it's all a part of defining my problem. If C actually took place before B, it changes the facts. I like to frame the facts, making sure they are in proper sequence. Then, it's like doing the puzzle. If there's a hole in the middle, I'm missing a fact. I know what it looks like, so I go looking for a fact that fits. Pretty soon I've completed this jigsaw puzzle and it's a picture of the whole thing. Now I own the problem.

"Scotty, there are two reasons why this method can fail. One is incomplete gathering of the facts. If I'm too lazy to gather anything but low-hanging fruit, I can't complete the jigsaw and I get the wrong answer. Second is getting the facts out of sequence. Great problem solvers are futuristic and they anticipate consequences. That's why I have to sequence the elements."

As I fished for the club she'd want on the next drive, I was thinking about George. Visual thinker that he was, he would love this jigsaw puzzle analogy.

"I heard a friend talking about problems and he said, 'You don't have a problem until you can define it,'" I offered, handing her an 9-iron.

"Absolutely. You took the words right out of the State Department handbook. Step one is called definition. If I can't define it or it isn't worth defining, go on down the road," Falona said. "And it has to be organized, otherwise it's just pieces in a heap."

She was silent as she looked straight at the green and swung.

The ball cut through the humid, thick air in a perfect arc. Satisfied, she handed the club back to me.

"The problem," she went on, "is that most people solve a problem based on the first information they get. They are linear problem solvers. But that just creates another problem down the line. In my construct, I get everything from all parties. That's crucial. If I have to adjudicate an argument, I'd better take all the time I need to get all sides. Otherwise, I'll linearly solve each problem. We had a President of this country who tried to do that. He didn't solve the problem systematically; he tried to solve it politically and that means pandering to either the first voice or loudest voice or the current voice. As Ben Franklin said, 'he who pleases all, pleases none.' It takes courage to be a problem solver.

"Scotty, I've been rattling on about problem solving. Now I've got a problem I'd like you to help me with. I can't seem to get these short chip shots near the hole. Can you help me?"

Caddies are asked lots of questions. Most of them are rhetorical. The valuable data we are expected to dispense is yardage to the green or to the flag or how carry to or over a hazard. Now typical golfers don't really know how far they can hit a particular club, and they are generally inconsistent anyway, but blame is easily shifted to the caddie when the golfers believe they have chosen the wrong club.

I could tell that Ms. Falona really wanted help, and frankly, she needed it. Her problem was the same that many high handicappers have — she tended to decelerate her club on short shots. Instead of a short backswing and accelerating through the ball, she tried to govern her distance by slowing the club down right before impact. Result: the dreaded chili-dip. Clubhead weakly stubbed into the turf with the ball barely getting airborne.

We had a minute or two before we could tee off so I took Ms.

Falona and three balls off to the side for a quick lesson. I suggested she open her stance slightly, take the club back along the target line, use a short backswing and crisply strike the ball letting the loft of the club do its thing.

"Ms. Falona, try to keep your eyes focused on the spot where the ball was until you hear it hit," was my last piece of advice. I placed the three balls in a row and moved back about 15 paces and asked her to try those suggestions.

Pop. Pop. Pop. All three landed within five feet of me with a gentle arc that would have nestled the ball near the hole had she been chipping toward a green.

"Hey, Scotty. That's great. I'll bet that saves me 5 strokes a round. Okay, back to the jigsaw method. I can see the whole thing and I can definitely see what I left out. This jigsaw puzzle is not two-dimensional. It's three-dimensional and sometimes four because time is added. And I've had problems where I could not get the facts to sit still. Things kept changing because people from the outside with vested interests were manipulating the facts.

"Step one: I get the facts so I have ownership of the problem. Step two: I decide that it is worth solving. Lots of times I won't know until I get the facts. Maybe it's not worth solving. Step three: I decide what my options are. I refrain from picking an option until I get all the options laid out. I get all options down, then I go through the process of thinking which one is right as opposed to which one I want to be right."

I nodded. This sounded familiar. "Kind of a smell test?"

"Yes, exactly. I have to detach myself from what I want the solution to be, so I don't detach myself from the truth. So which one is right? Which one will stand the smell test? What I do is think of the worst person in the world to find me wrong — a big client, the U.N. board — what if they saw me make a stupid mistake? They'd probably move their business elsewhere. Or I visualize the people whom this most affects and I know I owe them the time it takes to find the right answer."

I thought about the State Department story, and although I didn't know squat about Cuba, I figured whatever report she'd made was not what they'd wanted to hear. I asked, "How do you handle it when they rebuff your solution or when you arrive at it, you just know it isn't gonna fly?"

She offhandedly rubbed the side of her cleats with an already muddy towel. "I have to know," she said, "that I've arrived at the right answer because I've done it the correct way. Now, it takes courage sometimes — it might cost some money or some prestige — to solve the problem correctly. But I must be willing to call the hand. I have to be willing to say, 'Buddy, I'm sorry, but you have to know not to come to me with a problem, unless you want to hear reality. I don't know how to deal in nonreality.'

"I have learned the hard way that if I don't do it that way and I follow the line of least resistance in problem solving, then very shortly the problem will come back and hit me right on the nose. Hard."

I hadn't caddied for many women, but she was pretty good. She said it was just a hobby to help her relax and get in some walking, but I could tell that with some serious effort, she could be real golfer material. But she preferred just to take each hole as a new challenge, not paying much attention to her overall performance (she called it "existential golf"). I hadn't seen anyone play like that, but I had seen shabbier games. And by now I'd had worse company on the course, to be sure.

As we dodged the occasional puddle, she went on to talk about creative thinking. When she said the words, it gave me a knee-jerk bad reaction. Memories of Mrs. Trotter's horrid third grade classes filled my brain. They were so vivid I thought I could smell the glue pots and construction paper. I knew teachers who'd stressed "creative" this and that, but I never quite figured out what the standards were to differentiate say, creative writing from plain old writing. Never bothered to find out either, since I wasn't headed that way.

But Ms. Falona was talking about the kind of thinking that led you to be able to solve problems, to look for solutions. It also was the kind of thinking that could help you find a path to a goal, like O'Brien was talking about. I hadn't ever done it myself, so I was going to have to write it down and see if it worked. See if I could do it.

"I don't want you to think of creative thinking as something intangible or something only the artsy do. If you can learn how to do it, Scotty, then problem solving and other things become so much easier. I think anyone who follows the prescribed course of action can accomplish unbelievable feats of creative thinking. There's nothing mystical about it.

Now some people will have greater difficulty than others. Each human brain processes data differently. Some people are more analytical. They can process the facts but sometimes can't see the problem. An analytical mind often has to work harder. That sounds backwards, doesn't it? You've got to be mentally rebellious at times and the analytic often has a hard time letting go.

"It was beautiful to see the different types of intelligences that we used at the State Department. I saw it even more dramatically after I went to a think tank in Georgetown after the debacle. Scotty, there really are different types of genius. It's a crying shame that our schools don't recognize it."

"Ms. Falona, if you notice any particular genius that I exhibit would you please let me know so I can let my professors back home in on it?"

"Sure, Scotty, but I keep wandering off the subject. Let me get back to creative thinking and problem solving. What is required first is a conscious dedication to thinking — literally deciding to set aside time and think. I'm talking about conscious thinking. I don't mean the kind of thinking that goes on in our minds as we go about our day-to-day work. I'm talking about setting aside time to dwell consciously on a particular subject or problem, which ties in of course to problem solving. One of the facets of problem solving is determining your options. You also have to use creative thinking to develop options that are not self-evident."

This time she stopped. We stood and she continued, I guess so I would concentrate on what she was saying and not on avoiding patches of mud.

"There is a blank sheet. Let's say I need a solution or I need a new way to deal with someone. I need to be able to turn a client or an organization to a different conclusion. So I have something specific I want to accomplish. What I do — and what I suggest you try — is to carve out time to give this priority. To sit down and focus on whatever that subject is. Just dwell on it. Roll it through your mind. I've found that when I do menial tasks or physical tasks, that's a very good time for creative thinking because my mind isn't occupied by sweeping the deck. For me, it's playing golf.

"Now, if you have a creative bent, then all we're talking about is exercising some inherent God-given trait. But you can't depend upon that. So if you simply roll it through your mind with enough persistence, inevitably something will appear. A synapse will occur in your brain that creates a whole new thought.

"When I say rolling or mulling, I mean taking a situation and breaking it down as finitely as you can into its component parts. Now you have it in segments, as opposed to one big interlocked problem you're trying to creatively think through. So part of the mulling is pulling it apart and then walking around it, looking at all the angles. It's amazing. It truly is amazing. The answer will come out of the blue, but only because you've been focusing on it. You're wandering in the mental wilderness and all of a sudden: boom."

My first thought was that most problems I face — if I face them at all — are ones that need an immediate decision. Something that stresses me out. So I asked, "What if you're stressed and you have to decide right away? There's no luxury of time."

Ms. Falona nodded. "If you make this a habit, you'll be able to detach yourself enough to dwell on the problem without becoming more stressed. Don't let things intervene on your mulling time. If you're distracted, then it's not time to think.

"Secondly, in answer to your question, if it's urgent, here is my answer: I know that unless I do it this way, I'm not going to come up with the creative solution. If I am all wrapped up in emotion, anger, anxiety, whatever, it is not going to happen."

Although she hadn't kept score for herself, I figured Ms. Falona had shot a 96. As we made our way back to the clubhouse, I decided she'd not only shown me a different side of the game of golf, but a different approach to dilemmas and thinking through tough problems. So I stiffed her. Or I tried.

"C'mon, Scotty, you earned it. You were a patient and thoughtful caddie — more than I could have asked for," she insisted, trying to shove her money in my polo shirt pocket.

"No, I don't take a tip from someone who has taken the time to teach me something," I smirked. I was really beginning to like this part.

"Okay, then I'll have to make a donation in your name to my nonprofit organization. Your generous donation will help us further press freedom and eliminate human rights abuses by monitoring and reporting them. Thank you, Scotty."

Huh? I thought my consciousness had been raised a great deal already that summer, but this stuff was way out there. I was able to keep my eyes from rolling. "I don't object," I said. "Just be sure my contribution goes to the puzzle-solving department."

She smiled. "Consider it done."

While my fellow yahoos were slamming back brewskis outside the caddyshack (out of sight from the members, of course), I hurriedly wrote down Diane Taylor Falona's method of problem solving. **Step one: Define the problem.** Get all the facts and fit them together in jigsaw fashion. If you can't define it completely, don't go in. **Step two: Decide if it's worth solving.** Do you want to invest in this? Apply the old smell test. **Step three: Decide what your options are.** Lay them all out, even the seemingly stupid ones. Brainstorm and think creatively. **Step four: Solve.** Detach yourself from the emotion and stress and pick the option that IS the solution, not the one you WANT to be the solution.

I carried that tattered piece of my diary for years afterward — on the back was Bob's list of goal attainment steps. I used them both so much I didn't need them in written form anymore. But I kept running across people who did.

DISTANCE TO THE GREEN

JULY 5

Black Balls and White Balls

I'd had fun picking the brains of Jorgen, Diane and C.S. Case, but I was more than happy to hear O'Brien was back at National. He'd gotten in from Vegas yesterday, and Rich told me to meet him for his 8 a.m. tee-off.

When I saw him close his planner and hail me at the start of the course, I'd almost forgotten what a big, intimidating figure he was.

"Hey, Mr. O'Brien! Did you score big in Vegas?"

"Scotty, I never take what I can't afford to lose," he laughed.

I shouldered his bag and fell in step with him.

"Find you couldn't wire the craps table, Mr. O'Brien?" I asked facetiously. I wanted him to know I hadn't forgotten our last talk.

"Sometimes there's a thrill in just pure chance," he chuckled in his throaty way. "You might leave the dance with nothing in your pocket, but it was the dance that was the point."

"I'm not much of a gambling man myself," I admitted as he set up his tee. "Losing money isn't my idea of an ideal evening."

I really enjoyed caddying for Bob. The things we talked about were incredibly important, but as a golfer he was a pleasure to carry for. He was a very good, not great, player. He could be an outstanding golfer but he just didn't play often enough. What was really great about his play was that he played quickly. He had done all the pre-planning before he addressed the ball. There was just no mess around in the guy. He'd have his shot off before the typical player had finished fiddling with his grip. With Bob, it was a quick waggle and boom. The small breeze from the south that morning picked up what was already a hefty drive and carried it to a nice spot down the middle of the fairway. He'd set himself up to birdie the 1st hole.

He handed me his driver. "Scotty, losing is something you have to contend with sometimes. You make every effort to make sure it doesn't happen, but bad things happen. You just have to know how to handle them. I think of it in terms of black balls and white balls."

"Like pool?" I asked, handing him his iron.

"Sort of, but not quite. Scotty, good things happen occasionally, but bad things happen even more frequently. Think of the white balls as good news, the black balls as bad news, with shades in between. You have to know how to deal with both so that when one ball hits, you don't have to think then what to do about it. Have a plan.

"So you have black balls and white balls. It's really simple: When you get a white ball, the first thing you do is you pull it into yourself. You cherish it. You love it, you caress it and you protect it. There are predators out there who will take your white ball away from you because they shoot horses. So you put it inside your coat and tuck it away. It's a good deal. It's a date with a cute girl or a six-pack of beer that somebody left lying around. It's a white ball, right?

"A black ball is when something bad happens. You can think of an example — your girlfriend jilts you. An order that you took yesterday calls and they've been bought out. That was one you spent a lot of time on. Deal's off. The black ball, right? It's pretty easy to deal with white balls. The only thing you really need to do is to protect them. See, some people will take the white ball and yell, 'Hey! Look at my white ball!' Before you know it, it's a black ball because some other guy got himself a white ball, right? With black balls, though, you have to be more careful. If you've got more black balls than white balls and if a black ball has the same negative impact as a white ball has positive impact, within a very short time you could be down for the count. You're gonna get hit with black balls more than you're gonna get hit with white balls."

He flared his second shot and required a little bump and run shot to the green. "So how do you keep from getting hit hard with a black ball? You play baseball, Scotty?"

"I did in high school," I replied.

"Well, you know how to deal with the black balls then: You catch a black ball out in front of you with your arm extended. You put up a wall between you and a black ball — an emotional wall. And you don't let the black ball inside. It never gets into your body. You don't embrace it. It's out there someplace, and it's almost like your mind is detached from reality. You don't accept black balls in the sense that you don't let them in. You don't want to own the black ball."

It's really a good idea to run the ball towards most of the holes at National whenever you can. A lofted pitch shot is likely to kick off one of the numerous elephants buried in the greens. Those shots are very unpredictable and will careen off at some of the oddest angles, so a good chipper has the advantage. Bob bumped a 7-iron that ran about 60 feet and came to rest about eight feet from the hole. He drilled his putt firmly in the back of the cup for a workingman's par. I replaced the flag and then he gave me the most valuable advice about black balls.

"What you do with a black ball," O'Brien continued, "is you look at it and you try to make it white. It's amazing how many black balls are white balls in disguise. Lemons into lemonade. It's also amazing how many black balls you can take and throw at someone else, so they've got a black ball and you've got a white ball for having thrown it at them. You did that in school, but you could carry that to an extreme. You could take a black ball that was rightfully yours and pull a Judas Iscariot on it and say 'ain't my black ball, it belongs to Scotty. Scotty, here's the ball you left on my doorstep.' And all of a sudden I am the one yelling, 'Scotty's got a black ball!' because I gave it you. So you try to turn it into a white ball. If you can't, you drop it."

It sounded good in theory. But how could you really turn something bad into something good, I wondered. Then I remembered thinking my summer here was going to be a drag. But I wasn't the one who had made lemonade out of caddying at National. Well, maybe I had — with some serious help in the squeezing department — and hadn't realized what I'd done.

"But Mr. O'Brien, how can you do that? Turn something negative into a positive every time?"

As he addressed the ball on the tee at Number 2, he looked over his shoulder to give me what I now recognized as his pensive but cunning let-me-tell-you-a-story look.

"There was a guy named Heinz Durgen who owned Thompson Printing Company. He was German, spoke with a German accent. Carried himself ram-rod straight. One mean turkey. I mean tough. And I was trying to sell him an insurance policy — a big policy at the time. I was maybe 32, established but still a comer. It was a $1,000,000 policy. So I was giving him numbers and feeding him data tables, and he was getting the same from other people. I was in competition with other salesmen. This seemed to go on interminably. He was calling and I was giving him more numbers and more spread sheets. It went on for six months.

"So finally he called and he said, 'Bob, Heinz. Be here at 10 in the morning and we're going to settle this deal.' I said, 'Yes, sir, 10 o'clock. Your office.' So I showed up at 10 and there were seven other guys there. Seven insurance salesmen in his outer office. We were all looking at each other. The door opened and Heinz said, 'Come on in, fellas.' Called us all in his office together. Not one at a time — together. He turned to a fellow named Dave Rice who worked for one of my competitors. He said, 'Okay, Dave, why should I buy this from you?' Poor Dave went into this pitiful pitch. What the hell are you gonna say?

"So Heinz said, 'Okay, that's enough, Dave.' He cut him off. 'O'Brien.' Oh, no. Not Mr. O'Brien. Not Bob. 'What about you?' And I thought, I don't need this. No, a thousand times no. I said, 'Heinz, you son of a bitch.' He said, 'What?' I said, 'You son of a bitch. Here are eight grown men, professionals in what we do and you've got us dangling on a string like a bunch of puppets. And you want me to sit here and go through this charade. I'm not gonna do it. Good-bye.' He looked at me and he said, 'I'll be damned. Alright, the rest of you outta here.' I kid you not, Scotty. He said, 'Thank God. I've been waiting six months to find somebody worth buying this damn thing from.'"

I was in awe. "You said that to him?"

"Sure," he said. "He wasn't gonna buy from a guy who was gonna take a bunch of crap from him. He wasn't gonna do it and I don't blame him. And I walked out of there with the sale. All he wanted was someone to tell him to go to hell. Heinz Durgen was a huge black ball, but when I finished he was white as a virgin on her wedding day." O'Brien smiled at the memory.

"Old Heinz was tossing black balls around like they were doughnuts. I took his black ball and just threw it right back at him. And all of a sudden, he became a gigantic white ball. It was the same thing, Scotty. I refused to let the black ball he threw at me get into me. I said, 'No, I don't want your damn black ball. I'm outta here. I'd rather be gone than be stuck with ownership of your black ball. I don't want your black ball.' In that instance though, I didn't throw it back to him in anticipation that it would become a white ball. I threw it back to him only in that I refused to accept his black ball. The fact that it became a white ball was pure luck. I didn't anticipate that. It never entered my mind."

After parring the hole, O'Brien made his karate-chop motion that it was time to get moving. He took a 4-wood for the next tee and drove a beauty into the sun. The ball landed within breathing distance of the green.

"Scotty, do you remember when we talked about 'they shoot horses?'"

I nodded, remembering his father driven to the bottle.

"Good leaders don't kid themselves about that. Someone is ALWAYS waiting for you to mess up or for you to be vulnerable. I make every decision, personal and business, with that in the back of my mind. A lot of people get a sick joy out of seeing someone big choke — especially on his own ego."

It sounded a bit paranoid to me.

"Scotty, perception is reality. If people perceive that you are weak or that you aren't too bright, it's reality for them whether it's true or not. So you have to keep in mind that they will shoot you, given the opportunity. So shoot them first. Don't pull out your gun unless you intend to shoot. But if you have to, shoot them first. I shot Heinz before he could shoot me."

I've said that Bob was a fast player and that was absolutely true. But his swing was slow and smooth. He was a powerful man and to watch him hit a golf shot was to observe leverage in action. All of us have watched professional golfers and marveled at how far they can hit a ball with seemingly little effort. Of course, the secret of their success is simply one of physics. They are delivering terrific club head speed by maximizing all the simple machines that comprise the body working in unison. Bob's slow backswing created a powerful coil. His back turned away from the target, his hands moved far away from his head, and when he released that coil, his trunk and legs moved into the mix. The final kick was the release of the hands, wrist and forearms that really gave the clubhead its final velocity. When the ball is struck with this power and with precision, it is a thing of beauty and awe. Bob had all the elements of a superb game. His lack of practice and playing time reduced the precision part, but the power part was only diminished by the natural loss of flexibility that comes at age 55. His game was consistent and all came from his slow swing. It was like a Xerox. It always put him in the correct hitting position. If he had practiced more, he could've shaved another two or three strokes.

It really would have been fun to watch a match between Case and O'Brien. I wouldn't have wanted to have to chose for whom to caddie; I'd have been rooting for both. Both were in control, both focused and intense, and both super-competitive. Both knew how to keep the golf ball white, not black. They would not have beaten themselves by getting down after a hitting a poor shot. No, it would just have been the greatest day if they could have played for the fun of it and we could have tape recorded all their comments. That would have been a double-stiffing day, for sure.

I knew George would get a kick out of this black ball/white ball stuff. It was amazing how well it worked. Everything could be put into those two categories. Up to that point I was not thinking about it and I hadn't even realized the power of not accepting the black balls. They don't always turn into white ones, as O'Brien warned me, but I didn't need them either way. The awesome power of saying NO was another lesson he'd give me before the summer was out.

JULY 15

Pork

I've chosen July 15th as the point in my story about my summer at National to tell you about a really remarkable person who has had a big influence on me, Buck Ripkin. To this point my mentors have all been wealthy, powerful people. People who are used to deferential treatment, used to being waited on. Buck Ripkin was certainly not one of those types. No, Buck had been working for them for 40 years as a caddie at National. There are many remarkable things to tell you about Buck and his theories about people are every bit as valuable as those previously mentioned.

Buck was an African American raised in Florida during the dark days of segregation. Although a terrific student and athlete, the level of education available to Buck was only eight grades in an all-black, one-room schoolhouse. After that there were only a few segregated high schools and the closest was 28 miles from Buck's house. His options were working the cane fields or trying to arrange a way to attend high school.

During the summer after his eighth-grade year, he resigned himself to the cane fields. If you have ever spent any time in Florida in the summer, you know how brutally hot and humid it is. After the morning, Buck's hands were raw from swinging a machete. And the sun was only warming up for its afternoon punishment for anyone who dared test his resolve against it. At lunch, Buck took refuge from the heat under one of the few trees that could provide a little shade. One morning was enough to tell him that he couldn't do it — he had to find a way to attend that school. The Ripkins had family in the town where the high school was so Buck asked for their help. Although they had little room for him under the roof or at their table, they sacrificed to make it work. When Buck told me the story, he told me that was just the way it was in the Ripkin family: There was no hesitation to help the extended family.

As a young man, Buck was a tremendous basketball and baseball player. Of course, he knew nothing about golf. It would have been impossible for a man of color to play golf at that time and place. I saw Buck play the game several times that summer. In fact, I played with him in a Monday Caddie Best Ball, a monthly tournament which the caddies created on their day to play. Everyone would kick into the pot (winner take all) and then play a best ball. Your best ball score is the lowest of the two players of each team including their handicap. Not only did he know every inch of National and every break of every green from every angle, he could flat play the game. His powerful, smooth swing coupled with his knowledge of the course made him a fantastic partner. Given our handicaps, we were both deemed to be 3, I thought we wouldn't stand a chance against the notorious sandbaggers of the caddyshack. That day we both played very well and ham-and-egged it around the course, picking each other up when the other faltered. We finished 10 under par and picked up the $400 pot.

Buck, with the instruction and opportunities that I had, would have been on the tour. He was a great player, and at the time I played with him, he was in his 60s! This was a beautiful person. Always, and I mean always, Buck had a kind word and a smile. If Buck was your caddie, you would invariably play better than your usual game. He made you believe in yourself and your swing. If you worked with Buck on a given day, you were going to have some fun and the bag you carried always seemed lighter. Buck was easily the most requested caddie of us all. Rich had him booked days in advance and certain members wouldn't even play if they couldn't be assured that Buck was going to loop for them. Buck told me he had carried the bags of seven presidents of the United States. I'm sure he treated them all with respect, but I'm also sure they appreciated Buck's wisdom, sense of humor and storytelling. Buck's experiences on and off the course made him as valuable a shaman as any I met that summer. His metaphors were as memorable and illuminating as Bob O'Brien's.

Buck must have been around a pig farm in his youth because he had two memorable expressions about pork that he would use frequently. One was "Pigs get fat, hogs get slaughtered." Of course, that was his way of saying that fate has a way of taking down the greedy. At National, there were situations in every round when egos had to be checked so that players didn't go for a shot that was outside their capabilities or not a good percentage shot. The smart players play within the boundaries of their shot-making skills. If you "go for it" at National, unless you hit a miracle, you will pay. I've used that expression, "Pigs get fat, hogs get slaughtered" a thousand times since that summer. Pride and greed cometh before the fall.

The other porker remark Buck would use always cracked me up. We caddies got a lot of opportunities to share our insights during a round. If your player was hitting a shot from a spot near another player's, you'd always see the caddies sharing a few comments. At National there are several decision holes where the player has an option to lay up in front of water or go for it over the water. For many players, the decisions are no-brainers. They are either good enough to hit the shot or less skillful and know it and are content to lay-up and stay dry, at least temporarily. Given the egos of many members, you probably wouldn't be surprised to hear that many members had grand delusions about their skill levels.

Whenever Buck and I worked together and a member had opted to try to hit a shot beyond his abilities, Buck would always quietly say, "The pig is gonna try swimmin' again." We all know pigs can't swim and you can't teach them to swim. During one of the two times I carried for O'Brien when we played with others, Buck happened to be carrying. One of those situations occurred, just like I had mentioned. Well, Bob noticed me suppressing a laugh when Buck uttered his pig swimming comment and afterwards O'Brien asked me, "What was so damn funny right before I hit that ball into the lake?" So I repeated Buck's pig-swimming comment. Bob grimaced when he recognized himself as the bacon, but I could tell it set his mental wheels turning. The next time I carried for him, he had fully developed the "remedial pig swimming theory." I'm not sure Buck's message wasn't just as eloquent, but Bob had a fully-developed message that addressed the selection and utilization of personnel. It went like this:

"Scotty, I really like that expression that Buck used about pigs swimming. It got me to thinking about our people and the fact that they all have different talents. In fact, we all have different talents. You have talents I don't have, and I have some that you don't have. I don't care if it is environmental or hereditary. What happens in an organization is the tendency to take people and try to remake them in your own image even if they don't have the particular skills to adapt to your specifications. You hurt them and you can't take advantage of their strengths whatever they might be. This is a traditional and rigid way of managing. Try to make everyone out of the same cookie cutter. So what you wind up doing is that you are dealing in remedial swimming lessons for pigs. Pigs don't swim, right? You can give as many remedial swimming lessons as you want, but the fact of the matter is that pigs don't swim. The key to remedial swimming is to determine whether your swimming student is a pig, a rabbit, or a beaver. Beavers swim really well. So what is this person? Once you answer that, what are his or her skills? Then you build their function around their skills. Play to their strengths. You don't do remedial swimming lessons. Ever. You don't even invite pigs to the swimming meet, because all they'll do is get frustrated watching beavers swim.

"If you're building a company and you need beavers, go find beavers. Don't try to make a pig into a beaver. Not good. Another thing, these are not empty vessels we are talking about. You can't pour in what you want. The fact is that the vessel is already full and it is whatever it is. Pigs, beavers, garbage. It is virtually impossible to take out the bad stuff and put in the good. By the time we get most people, they are pretty much fully formed. That is why the selection process is so crucial. You have to hire the right people or you spend all your time and resources in remedial swimming lessons." I don't know if Buck appreciated how profound his pig-swimming comment was, but O'Brien had recognized it as a major theory of corporate development.

Another of Buck's observations and musings had to do with the energy level and activities of the members of the club. He had divided the population into two types depending on their energy. He said that some people were "sunrisers" and some were "sunsetters." Ol' Buck would look at a caddie, or a groundscrew member, or a busboy, or a member, and say, "Look at that man go! He sure is a sunriser." Or he would see a slacker, like a caddie who really wouldn't look for Richard to give him a bag on an especially hot afternoon, and Buck would point it out by saying, "Look at that member of the Sunset Club." I mentioned that to Bob just before he was leaving for another one of his gaming trips. "Scotty, that's another beauty. You know, we really see that in every company or every population of people. When I get back, let's talk about that."

Buck, like most of us, was also a student of the golfers' conversations. I can only imagine the things he'd heard over the years from the mouths of those whose bags he'd carried. But he had a phrase he used that seemed to sum things up. "No study, no speak," Buck would mutter under his breath when someone was out of line or said something ridiculous. If you don't know what you're talking about, you have no right to open your mouth. It's simple, but it's amazingly effective in the heat of debate when said to someone who has his facts mixed up. No study, no speak — end of story.

Buck Ripkin still inspires me. Buck was a handsome man and the way he carried himself was regal. His manner was beautifully paradoxical: incredibly proud and humble simultaneously. He had the same respect for mankind that Jorgen had. God, what a winning personality! Often I have wished I could live up to that standard. These are true gods who walk among us. They have grace. You meet people like this so rarely. Nurture and cherish those relationships.

As the summer wore on, I discovered more about Buck. He had played in the Negro Leagues for the Homestead Grays with Josh Gibson, had batted against Satchel Paige and had seen the young Jackie Robinson. I asked Buck if he was bitter about not being able to play in the Major Leagues. He set me straight.

"Bitter? Why, Scotty, those were the greatest times. We were just as good, better even, than the white fellas. In cities where we shared a stadium, we often outdrew them. In barnstorming exhibitions we beat their All-Star teams, including the Babe. My life was blessed. I had fun, I ate good, and the women was just as beautiful around our parks as theirs. No sir, I didn't have time to be bitter.

Pork

When Jackie went, I guess we knew our time was going to come to an end. That was a shame because it was a beautiful time. I worked here at National during the off season and I just loved the tranquillity of it. And when I discovered the game of golf, I fell in love with it. Now, if I am a little bitter, it's because I couldn't play this game when and where I wanted to. That was a pitiful situation."

Yes, it was. A pitiful situation.

DISTANCE to the GREEN

AUGUST 2

Be a Pipe - Not a Bucket

O'Brien was back at the club, and as always, he had Richard assign me to carry his bag. And I could tell the minute he greeted me on the putting green, he had something on his mind. As I approached with his bag which I had collected from the storage room, he was busy putting about a dozen balls four or five feet from one of the cups. Bob knew that two or three shots during the round would be saved if he converted putts from that distance. Statistics show that even the pros make fewer of those than the average player thinks. You rarely make a long snake, but the greater sin is to leave a lag putt outside of the tap-in range. Three putts kill your scorecard. The other aspect of the game that players fail to appreciate is the ability to get up and down from off the green. Even a player with a 10 handicap is likely to miss six or more greens in a round. That places a premium on chipping and making the four- to six-foot putt.

So Bob's routine was to finish his putting practice with a few long ones just to get the speed of the green. By practicing the crucial four-footer, Bob established the accuracy of his stroke. He did two things especially well that made him consistent. First, he absolutely did NOT move his head, and therefore his shoulders, in his stroke. That is death to the short putt. I swear it seemed like he kept his gaze down until he heard the ball rattle in the cup. Second, there was very little wrist action in his stroke. Again that provided an element of consistency that was always there for him.

I could tell he was anxious to expand on Buck's comments. He was practically bounding across the green to shake my hand. "Scotty, Buck's comment about the nature of people was right on. There really are two types of people, and it's not urgency we are talking about. It's a bias towards action. I don't know if it is learned or not, but it darn sure isn't there in everyone. If you can figure out what kind of person you are dealing with, it can make a difference. It is really important if you couple Buck's theory with his remedial pig swimming theory. If you are able to determine that a person whom you are counting on doesn't have this bias to action, you had better find him a place as a doorstop or a paperweight or get him out the door.

"At rest is a natural state for some people. They're perfectly comfortable watching a ballgame on TV, knowing they'll take the trash out later. For those people, it makes no sense to take out the trash while the game is on, that's irrational and unnatural. But the person with a bias for action is just the opposite. His natural state is action. Attack. Move. Go. Start. Run. Hit. Whatever it is he's doing. He is compelled to action. I mean that in a literal sense: It is a compulsion. That can become a weapon to be used against yourself because you become a workaholic. It just isn't any fun to be around people like that — they wear you out. And they don't give themselves any slack.

"And you know it's not simply energy, either. A biased-to-action person can be dog-tired and still compelled to keep going. Some people are naturally at rest and must leave that homebase in order to go into action. Others leave a state of action to go at rest. The most successful ones are the latter who have learned not to carry this too far — to go at rest frequently enough to refresh themselves, enjoy life."

That sounded exactly like Christopher Schnebly Case. No, actually that was Chief Harry Coolwater talking about harmony.

"Mr. O'Brien, that sounds like a physics law I studied last year. Things at rest stay at rest, things in motion tend to stay in motion. I think it has something to do with inertia."

"Precisely. That's a good correlation. Let's say you possess this bias to action and you can use it as a tool and not as a weapon against yourself. What have you got? And I don't mean just selling."

"Well, Mr. O'Brien, I guess if you are 'hyper' like that and you can channel it, you are really going to get a lot accomplished. I mean, I would hate to compete against a guy like that. You figure he is going to outdo you at anything."

"Right you are, Scotty. He will beat you at mowing the grass, selling things, winning friends. This person will accomplish more. He will be in action when the rest are still sitting in their hammocks.

"Let's take two opposites — one naturally at rest, one naturally in action. Let's say that the one who is at rest is able to discipline himself to leave the natural state and go in action. And the one who is naturally in action is able to abate his compulsion, so the two of them are performing at the same pace. You would think they would both be seen and be determined to be equal. I have learned that the action-oriented one who is holding back will be viewed by his peer group far superiorly. Instinctively, you can tell whether the person is leaving action to go at rest versus leaving rest to go into action. People like to be associated with people whose natural state is 'get it done.' We trust them. We are willing to turn our affairs over to them. There's no chance it's not gonna get done on time and correctly. This is particularly true in selling. A buyer loves to have people on his team who he knows are working for him even while he is asleep. And he doesn't worry that while he is working, they're taking a nap someplace."

"Mr. O'Brien, does this difference between the two people you're talking about have something to do with their capacity for action?"

"Scotty, that's brilliant! The 'action person' has another gear to shift into if he needs it. And I suppose it's there to behold. It really is comforting to know that the person you are dealing with still has something in the tank. Yep, I think you're on to something."

"So these people with a bias to action are potential workaholics?"

"They can be and, of course, the danger is that they will become runaway engines. They either burnout or have a heart attack."

"Mr. O'Brien, are you a workaholic?"

"What do you think, Scotty?"

"I don't think so. You seem to be able to turn the dial down when you need to."

"When I go at rest, I am really at rest. I don't have any problem once I say it's time to quit. Where I do have a problem is making myself go at rest when there's something still to be done. So I plan my work, my functions around urgency, around getting things done. But when I go on vacation for a month, I never call the office. That's unnatural for an attacking workaholic. He'll call in from Bora-Bora. I don't call in. Ever."

"Mr. O'Brien, I'll bet you're one of those people who is on the go even when he's on vacation."

"Oh, no, Scotty. On the contrary. I love to cruise and I especially like the transatlantic over the island hop variety. Nope, give me my deck chair and about 10 books and leave me alone. I just love to sit on my veranda and watch the horizon go by. This differentiates me from the true workaholic and allows me the time to contemplate. I need that time for planning. When everything is urgent, you don't have the time to back off so you can do that."

"So, have you specifically tried to hire people for your company who have a bias to action? And if so, how can you tell what tendency the person has?"

"Oh, yes, we absolutely try to find these people, and let me tell you, they are not easy to identify. Everybody wants to hire them. But I look at the background of accomplishments. That will tell you a great deal. There is another technique I like to use after a successful interview. Let's say that during the interview we are on the same wave length, so I say, 'I really enjoyed this. Let's get back together next Tuesday...' within a fairly short time frame. No more than three days. Then I'll ask, 'Would you do me a favor? Would you summarize in a memo what you and I have talked about? Then, as we're moving down the trail, we'll know where we've been.' Now the key is to see if the summary is done when we get back together and done in its entirety. If it's not, there's no bias to action."

"I get the feeling that this bias to action is about more than just physical activity."

"Oh, most definitely. Bias to action has to do with performing — and the action is whatever needs to be done. It could easily be thinking. That's action, though not physical. It takes a great deal of energy to sit and think.

"Now, I should say very few people are 100 percent one way or the other. Most people are about 60/40 towards non-action. Maybe 65/35. If this person works for you, you've got to think about remedial swimming. Can you get him up to a state of action that will be valuable? Then it becomes a question of leadership. If he perceives that you as the leader expect action and he wants your love, he will begin to develop a greater bias to action. He either sees the value of this course of action or he realizes that you ain't gonna take him with you on the journey. That's the most effective way to modify that sort of behavior or inactivity. But it doesn't always work, and you know they shoot horses, don't they?"

"Mr. O'Brien, how do I know if I've got it? And what do I do with it?"

"Well, Scotty, I think you've got it. I don't know if you know you have it, but knowing that and relying on it can really make a difference. Here's how. First, never ever follow a leader who does not have a bias to action. He'll leave you stranded half way to Chicago. He may have a great concept but without the commitment to follow through, you are not going to get there. The other important thing you derive out of this self-awareness is the quiet confidence that you'll have in yourself when you know that your bias to action is a tool for success. Then if you couple it with goal attainment, shoot, you're a natural-born, modern miracle of success."

Man, I was ready to leap a tall building with a single bound after that. I could see why Bob had been so successful, but as we moved from the putting green where we had been temporarily stranded, he really brought it all into shape. National does not have tee times, so the few groups who normally would have been behind us had teed off while we were on the practice green. I knew that our pace was going to be slower than normal.

"Scotty, the corollary to bias to action is a cornerstone of my business success. The thing that goes hand in hand with it is this: Be a pipe not a bucket. It is how I built my company 35 years ago. On a piece of black paper, using goldleaf typewriter ribbon, I typed the words: Don't fill up your bucket. Do not limit yourself to your own capacity. That's why I decided not to become a practicing lawyer, because you have only so many hours in the day, and you can bill only so many hours. You know, the perfect example of this is Tom Sawyer and the story of whitewashing the fence. Every kid has heard it or read it, but almost nobody gets the real meaning. I was amazed when I first read it and discussed it in school that my classmates — the herd — thought the story was how cleverly Tom had gotten out of work. He was able to sit down and relax, rest and get others to do his job. Now, what I got out of the story was that Tom had multiplied himself, and in so doing, conserved part of the energy he innately had. Therefore, he exponentially expanded his energy. He became a pipe, not a bucket. He moved it on down."

"Come on, Mr. O'Brien, you really saw that story that way in grade school?"

"Scotty, I kid you not. I thought it was beautiful what Tom had done. He had created synergy. I didn't use that word nor did I call it being a pipe, but I knew I was on to something and I can give you an illustration to that effect."

By now we had teed off, and with Bob setting his usual quick pace, we were waiting on the group ahead of us. I could sense Bob's impatience. He really did have a bias to action. He became perceptively agitated. Hitching his pants, taking extra practice swings, twisting his trunk to loosen his back muscles. I could tell something was going to give.

"Scotty, let's go. Follow me."

He snatched up his ball and set off on a bee line through a small thicket of woods. Bob evidently had done this before. We crossed over a small creek, up over a little rise, and popped out about 60 yards from the 4th green. Bob then rolled his ball out on the fairway. I silently flipped him his wedge and, as he popped the ball on the green, we heard one of the groups that had been ahead of us teeing off on 4, now behind us.

"As I was saying, when I was a kid, they held the annual Soapbox Derby out at Swope Park. This Italian fellow had the ice cream concession. He could hire only so many guys to sell for him because he had a certain number of these little push carts that had fudge bars and popsicles and stuff. I think he had 10 carts all together. But I got on — I had one of the 10 carts and we roamed up and down where the people were watching the Derby selling these ice cream bars. Well, it was a warm day and business was good. The Tom Sawyer thing was fresh in my mind, so I took some old milk cartons — you know, the kind the milk man put your milk in on your porch to keep it cold — and made about 10 of these things that could hold ice cream bars and keep them cold. So I became a middle man. I was a wholesaler.

"About every 10 minutes I'd be back at the tent filling up my cart with ice cream. The fellow was counting the money and after the second time I came in, he noticed I was back again for another load of ice cream. He said, 'What the hell are you doing?' I said, 'I'm selling ice cream.' He said, 'You got a scam going, don't ya?' I said, 'I don't have a scam going. I am selling ice cream.' He said, 'No problem, kid, just make sure the money comes out in the end. I'm watching you.' I said, 'Not to worry.'

"So I got my 10 guys and I was sitting there around the corner. They were selling ice cream. Worked like a charm. Here's the point: Do everything you can not to fill up your own bucket, because if you fill it up, you have no place to go. You're full. Two things happen. First, when you're full, you're maxed out. You can't take on any more. No matter how good the opportunity is, you're maxed out. Second, and more important, sludge drops to the bottom. The good stuff rises to the top and then starts spilling out over the sides. They're buying from someone else because you couldn't get there. Now pretty soon, you have a bucket full of sludge, garbage. A better metaphor is not to be a bucket at all. Do what I did at Swope Park with the ice cream and what Tom Sawyer did: Be a pipe. Move things along so you'll always have room for the good stuff. Your capacity is infinite!"

By this time, we had left the group we jumped ahead of on 4 far behind. National is really a gorgeous place and because it is mature, each hole is separate and distinct and isolated from the others. Typically, the spacing between groups is such that you never see anyone else while you are on the course. The course really isn't that busy either. The typical publinx will have 50,000 rounds of golf per year played on it. National will see maybe 8,000. Because of that and its incredible maintenance, National is as perfect a place to play as can be found anywhere. The only possibility for a less than perfect lie is in a divot. That's hard to find because the grounds crew is continually and constantly filling the divots with a green mixture of sand and seed. The course is completely closed when the weather is severe, from mid-November to mid-February. The year-round caddies either have maintenance jobs at National or moonlight during that part of the year.

O'Brien and I made record time on the round. He was playing a little faster than usual because of his travel plans that afternoon. He probably had no business being out on the course that morning, and I'm sure his wife worked him over for playing golf on the morning he was supposed to be packing for a 10-day cruise in the Mediterranean. But Bob was a doer...he had a bias to action and he saw no reason not to squeeze in one more activity before he took a rest.

DISTANCE to the GREEN

AUGUST 20

Paradox of Risk

I had really looked forward to this day. My favorite mentor, O'Brien, was scheduled to be back at National for a couple of days following his cruise. I knew he would have some great stories to tell and I hoped to add lessons into my ever-growing storehouse of truths. As usual, Bob wanted to play early and alone. Richard was accommodating and warned me the night before that O'Brien was teeing off at 6:45 a.m. At that time of the morning, we would be lucky if the mowing crew could stay ahead of us.

O'Brien did not disappoint me. I greeted him cordially and with more familiarity than my first meetings, "Hi, Mr. O'Brien. How was the cruise?"

"Scotty, it was marvelous and you won't believe what happened in Rome. I had an experience that was an extreme example of 'executive action.'"

"What do you mean, 'executive action?'"

"Scotty, do you remember when we talked about goal attainment?"

How could I forget? I had been trying to live those five steps ever since.

"Well," he continued, "by executive action, I guess I am referring to steps four and five: Commit and do it, combined with bias to action. It's that instinct that says something needs to be done right now or an opportunity will be missed."

"Sure," I said, "you mean that non-academic, anti-beer talk, sort of John Wayne approach."

"Yeah, John Wayne. That's good, Scotty. But this 'executive action' is really a super-compressed version of the process we discussed in goal attainment. It really is about training yourself to make instant decisions when required. And that scenario happens constantly in life and business. This instant, reactive decision-making skill is really vital in moving stuff along.

"This probably sounds vague, but so often I see people plagued by the inability to decide. Executive action is the ability to instantaneously size up a situation or an opportunity, subconsciously make a call, and then act. It isn't necessarily the process you would use to decide a big deal or a business plan or whom you marry, but it really is beautiful when you need to make a quick decision. As you will see from my illustration, it is intuitive and instinctive. Executive action is something you learn to trust through experience and repeated validation. But let me tell you what happened, and you can see where I'm coming from.

"My wife, Mary Jo, our son John and I were in Rome together during this last trip. We met in Paris. John is between college and law school. We were taking him to the train station so he could get back to England. Mary Jo and I were going to the Vatican. When we got to the train station, the train was sold out so John decided to join us on our trip to the Vatican. John suggested we take the subway, which he said was something everyone should try at least once. Now he's looking at this from the perspective of a 20-year-old in blue jeans who is up for adventure. He's not looking at it from the perspective of a 55-year-old and his wife, dressed to the nines. But now we are going into the bowels of the Roman subway system where who knows whom we could meet."

We'd reached the 1st tee box. It was a gorgeous morning. Light breeze from the south, not a cloud in the sky.

"Here's your driver. So you are dressed for the Vatican but have decided to take the subway." I had never been to Rome, but I was starting to see the scene.

"Right," O'Brien said. "There was an underground right there at the Rome train station. So off we went. It was packed. I mean the humanity down there is real — very fragrant. No, Scotty, it stinks! So we got down there and crowded onto the subway. The good news was that I was bigger than anyone around. The average passenger was five-seven and I had eight inches on most of 'em.

"The hustle and bustle was bothering me but I was keeping my eye on Mary Jo and John, who had his backpack and everything. And I saw this little gypsy lady board the train with her ragamuffin kids. They were all layered in their chocolate-colored clothes. I saw her get on but as the doors began to close I watched her slip off. It all happened in a matter of just a few seconds. I carry my credit card case in my right front pocket. And in my left front pocket I have my money clip. I reached for my credit card case and it was gone."

O'Brien hit his tee ball with its usual left-right fade, down the middle about 250. "Nice ball," I remarked as we moved down the dew-sprinkled fairway.

"So I knew instinctively there was no time for analytics or to think things over, or she'd be gone. I was off that subway and from the time I saw her get off there was no time for to-the-surface analytics. It was all taking place cerebrally — I was unconsciously thinking. I got off, barely squeaking through the closing doors. By then the gypsy lady was about five feet away and she was sauntering because she thought she just made a big score."

"Mr. O'Brien, I think it's a 5-iron."

"Thanks, Scotty. Now I wasn't sure she had my credit card case because I didn't see her take it. So I was faced with the dilemma of confronting her or getting back on the train and surrendering my credit cards. But I was not thinking that at any conscious level. If my brain was processing and making choices, it was doing it out of sight from my rational mind. I knew darn well she had done that a thousand times and would deny everything. So I went up behind her and grabbed her by the scruff of her coat. I spun her around and I said, 'Give me the goods.' Well, of course, she went nuts, started yelling, and so I said, 'Give me the goods or I'll throw you under the train.'

Bob's 5-iron stopped about 25 feet from the hole. I handed him his putter. He never broke stride in the telling of the story.

"At that point, I saw my credit card case fall out on the deck of the platform. Luckily it didn't fall in the crevice between the train and the five-foot drop to the tracks. So I flung her aside — and by that time a crowd had gathered around — and I heard whistles blowing and police coming from above. I reached down, picked up the card case, jumped back on the subway — John had been holding the door — and away we went. The whole thing took about 10 seconds. From the look on Mary Jo's face, it must have seemed like 10 minutes. She had an expression of both panic and relief. So I was back on the train, with my card case, and the crowd just parted. The big fat gringo was back."

"John Wayne, eh, Mr. O'Brien?"

"One guy who spoke English said, 'She got your wallet, huh?' I said, 'Yeah, well, I got it back.' He said, 'What??' I said, 'Oh, yeah!' He said, 'How did you know she had it?' I said, 'I didn't, but if not her, who?' He said, 'Well, I'll be a son of a bitch.' So my point is that executive action is sometimes the thing you do when you have to react instinctively. It's urgent and you don't have time to think it through. You go with your gut reaction because those reactions have always been your friend."

Just about that moment, O'Brien's 25-foot putt curled into the hole for a birdie. I whistled and remarked, "Nice no-brainer, Mr. O'Brien."

"Scotty, sometimes things just vector together. They just come. As I tell people whom I train, my word for it is 'executive analytics.' But I have found it is extremely difficult to teach. Bringing the pieces and the parts together so that you can mobilize in that blink of an eye is easier said than done. If you have the luxury of time you can run through all the iterations and scenarios and then you use the uncompressed version of goal attainment.

"Scotty, here's my point on 'commit and do it.' I see several types of people every day. Some come to the right conclusion about what should be done whether it's instantaneous or thought out, but they don't do anything with the right answer. Then I see other people act. The problem is, they don't have the right answer. They are just ready, fire, aim. Sometimes they are fire, ready, aim. The trick is to have a process that will carry you through the labyrinth, that will tell you what to do and then have that attack mode that is beyond urgent. It is compulsive. When you put those two together, then you have a formidable weapon. Not only do you know what to do, you're prepared to execute it. At once. Or you're prepared to go home, go take a nap, go have a beer."

Our round continued, and he was a hot golfer that morning. I mean sizzling. Bob was capable of putting up good numbers, but he was uncanny that morning. After five holes, he was 1 under par. Two birdies, 2 pars and a bogey. He was ebullient and talkative. I found his dissertations on life spellbinding, and I knew with little prompting I was going to get a world-class lesson today.

"Scotty, I might have mentioned to you earlier that winners win. I have given this a lot of thought over the years. Some people have attributed my success to just dumb luck and, frankly, a few times that might have been the case. But year after year, time after time, you start to develop an independent theory of why things turn out the way they do."

"Mr. O'Brien, I remember during a round a month ago that you let me in on a secret that went something like — if it isn't wired, don't go. I think you called it the '**paradox of risk**.'"

"Good memory, Scotty. And I have been thinking some more about that conversation we had. We decided that winners win or certainly tend to win. And losers lose or tend to lose. When a winner loses, it's an aberration. The common belief is that the winner wins because he is a winner. My belief is contrary, the opposite. He wins, therefore he IS a winner. As I've said, I think he wins for a simple reason: He wins because he never goes into battle unless he has it wired. That's why he wins. The winner knows he has the edge and knows what is going to happen.

"That reminds me of an event early in my business career. This goes back to a time when our operation was a fledgling. Things were going well and we were looking to expand our office space, which at the time was in one of the large bank buildings. So the bank president, along with the building manager and several of their veeps, invited me to dinner with several other business people. I'm sure I was the youngest person there. They gave us — I still have it — a block of wood that was the stand for a silver dollar. It had my name on it and served as my place card. The silver dollar could be twirled around on a spindle. So, of course, while all the scintillating dinner conversation was swirling around me, I played with it.

"Coincidentally, the building manager and I were in negotiations over new space in his building. I wanted the walls in our office entryway to have true tongue-and-groove walnut paneling.

He wanted walnut plywood trimmed with walnut one-by-fours. A lot cheaper and it looks exactly what it is: walnut plywood trimmed with one-by-fours. I was getting nowhere because I had no leverage.

"So, as I was playing with this silver dollar on the pedestal, I noticed that the split washer that helped suspend the dollar in the cradle was positioned so a slight amount of friction was created between it and the dollar. Anyway, when you spun the dollar and as it slowed, invariably it came up heads. The deal was wired. I said to the building manager, 'I'll tell you what we'll do. You spin this silver dollar and if it's heads, I get tongue-and-groove; if it's tails, we'll do the plywood.'

"Well, he was a macho guy and we were in front of a bunch of people including the president of the bank, who was a super-macho guy. So he said, 'Sure.' Obviously, I got the tongue-and-groove paneling. I already had it wired. I was the winner. That might not be a perfect example of goal attainment because it was truly rigged, but in a way it is a very good example because I studied the odds before I made any move. As in any business deal, he had the same opportunity to study the situation. Going back to our goal attainment process, I had an objective and I had figured out a way to wire it."

The concept of removing chance from the equation struck me as contrary to the American Dream, so I asked, "Mr. O'Brien, are you saying that luck isn't involved?"

"Scotty, when you see a guy who has a Midas touch, it is NOT luck. He has it wired. I'll tell you again — this point is far more important than it appears because it so obvious: If you can't wire an important deal, don't do it. Just say no.

"Most people never figure this out. If you talk to them about me, they'll say something like, 'O'Brien is the luckiest guy around. Every time he sets his sights, it works.' That's because I don't tell them about the other eight deals I looked at but couldn't figure out a way to make them work. So I passed. I only put the bet down when I know the odds are dramatically in my favor. Then, remember Scotty, COMMIT. Bet the pot, if necessary."

The incredible education I was obtaining was pushing my golf obsession aside. When I had left home seven weeks earlier, I had a moderate interest in being associated with the golf mecca that is National. I had a terrible attitude about leaving my male and female friends behind for the summer. Now I was feeling that I was in precisely the right place at precisely the right time. I wanted this round of golf to go on for 10 hours. Of course, with Bob's relentless pace we were chewing up the real estate. We had completed the front 9 in about 90 minutes. O'Brien was having the round of his life. He was on auto-pilot, his conscious mind freed from the game itself. That allowed him to truly "get into the zone." We had an expression for it on the college golf team. We called it "feelin' golfy." That's the feeling that doesn't come often enough when you put everything out of your mind except firing at the pins. No negative thoughts. The fairway looks like it's 100 yards wide when you tee off. Your approach shots to the green are routine, in fact, you start shooting for specific parts of the green: back right or front left, depending on the placement. The line of the putt is so obvious it's like the runway lights at the airport at night, guiding your ball right into the cup. Well, O'Brien was feeling real golfy.

But Bob was also just superstitious enough not to make much of it. I know he had never made the turn at National 1 under par before.

As he prepared his tee shot on 10, I could sense a light going on in his head.

"Scotty, I just remembered a marvelous story about a coin flip that I have got to share with you. This one did not involve a defective spinner on a place card. It was a flip for about $400,000."

"Mr. O'Brien, I thought I heard you say it was for $400,000."

"You heard right, my boy. That was a doozy."

"Unless you had a two-headed coin, I don't know how you could wire that deal."

"You're right, the $400,000 flip couldn't be completely wired. But it was only part of a larger transaction that had reached an impasse requiring drastic action. Plus I was feeling lucky. Like today."

No sooner had those words left his lips than he hooked his drive right into a fairway bunker and the ball was buried beneath the lip of that trap. From there all he would be able to do is chip back onto the fairway with his wedge. Normally, Bob was pretty impassive after a mistake on the golf course, but this had been a special round so I wasn't surprised to see him express some emotion.

"Damn. I knew I shouldn't have let the golf gods hear me say that. Let me give you the background leading up to the coin flip. The more I think about it, maybe this is about winners winning. It's also a great story about intuitively sizing up your adversary."

Using his wedge, Bob hit his second shot back on to the fairway. He still had 195 yards to the green. The wind was in our faces for the third shot.

"Mr. O'Brien, how 'bout a 3-iron knock down shot?"

He looked back at me somewhat quizzically, but nodded. He then preceded to smoke that 3-iron right at the flag stick. The knock down shot has a low follow through that keeps the trajectory of the shot lower, thereby minimizing the effects of the breeze. His shot caught the front part of the green. Fortunately, the pin placement that day was in the back so that when the shot stopped rolling, he was only 12 feet right of the cup. O'Brien grinned.

"The circumstances surrounding the coin flip were fairly straight forward. The stalemate was about money, of course. We had entered into a contract with a major corporation and the hang up was about the interpretation of the contract. Naturally, when a contract is involved, lawyers are involved. Well, he had two lawyers and I had mine. And we were going around and around and inevitably coming back to same place: nowhere.

"Scotty, one thing about CEOs of big deal companies is that usually they have fairly large egos and, secondly, they aren't used to hearing 'no.' They just don't have much experience in dealing with 'no.' In selling, the easiest sale is to the CEO. The hardest sale is to the purchasing manager. The purchasing manager is a professional buyer and a professional sayer of 'no.' The CEO is an amateur buyer — he seldom buys. He makes decisions, but he can be romanced, he can be ego-ed.

"This was a situation where neither of us was going to budge an inch. Our macho egos were in full bloom, and it became more than just the money. Now this part of the contract was only part of the deal, so the $400,000 part was not as important to me as getting by this sticking point and moving on."

Bob's putt was a tricky, side hill putt that would break left to right, which is usually harder for a right-handed putter to read. I figured if he made this for par he was still golfy, but if he missed, maybe the golf gods were working to even the score a bit.

The greens at National were like glass. During that time of the summer, they were super quick, probably 11 on the stimpmeter, so all Bob had to do was to get the ball rolling and gravity would do the rest. I read the break to be about 18 inches. This was one tough putt. Bob struck the ball on the end of the putter blade to deaden the impact even more. In putting, it is important not to decelerate the putter even with short or delicate putts. Bob's touch was uncanny that day. His read was perfect, but as the putt curled towards the hole, I thought he had left it on the high side. At the last possible moment the ball lost almost all of its forward momentum and died with that beautiful sound that only a ball rattling into the cup can make.

"Great sandy," I remarked.

Bob knew better than to test the golf gods again, so his only reaction was a slight smile. The coin flip story continued.

"As I was saying, Scotty, I was struck by an inspiration at that moment of the impasse. I simply said to the lawyers, 'Why don't you guys step outside? I want to talk to Craig privately.' I'll never forget, Craig's lawyers looked at him and he said, 'Yeah, Bob and I want to talk privately.' So they stepped outside and I turned to Craig and said 'Craig, both of us are too strong-willed to give in on this.' And of course he said, 'I know I am not going to give in.' And I said, 'It ain't likely I am going to give in either. So we need to find another way around it.' He said, 'Got any ideas?' 'Yeah,' I said, 'I'm gonna say this because I know this will meet our need. I'll flip you for it.' He said, 'What??' I said, 'I'll flip you for it.'"

"Mr. O'Brien, how much did you say this was for?" I asked.

"Oh, this was worth, maybe $400,000. He said, 'People will think we're crazy.' I said, 'No, they already think we're crazy. But you know it's like the shoot-out at the OK Corral. I'll just flip you for it. To hell with it.' He said, 'You'd really do that?' 'Hell, yes,' I said, 'in a New York second.' So he said, 'Yeah, why the hell not?'

"I pulled out a quarter and asked him if he wanted to use two coins or if he just wanted to use one. He said to use the quarter, that he would call it in the air, but to make sure that I let it hit the floor. I said, 'Bet on it' and flipped the coin. He called heads. It landed tails. I looked at him and said, 'Looks like I am taking

$400,000.' He said, 'Looks like it.' So we called the lawyers back in and Craig said proudly, 'We resolved it. Bob wins. Go get Bob's money.' His lawyer shook his head, 'Craig, I thought you'd never give in.' Craig said, 'I didn't give in. We flipped for it.'

"Scotty, ego is the incredible motivator. I had a hunch, no check that, I knew that the gunslinger part of Craig's ego would help me break the impasse. Hell, he was nearly bustin' with himself when he let those lawyers know we had settled it like men out in the street. It nearly took all the sting out of losing the $400,000."

"Did he come through with the dough?" I asked.

"You bet he did. It would have broken the code of West to do otherwise. In fact, we went on to do some other deals after that.

"This logjam that Craig and I hit reminds me of a bromide of mine that we talked about earlier this summer. Do you remember when we discussed the ability to say no?"

Of course I did. It had been an integral part of the heavy chats that George and I had at the NuWay. I nodded yes.

"Well, there is an important corollary to that which I call 'never take a maybe.'"

Again, I must have had that confounded look on my face, because Bob asked, "Going too fast for you, Scotty?"

I have to admit my head was fairly spinning, but I was game and couldn't wait to get to the NuWay that night to share my new-found gems with George. At our current pace of play, we would finish in about an hour and Bob would set his own personal best score at National.

"Scotty, I'm going to try to tie some of this together for you. You've heard me talk about some success we have had over the years and that many people ascribe that sort of success to luck or a tolerance for risk. And you've also heard me say that's hogwash, and that I am not a true risk-taker in the classic sense. I'm not going to put something of value at risk where the odds aren't really heavily tilted in my favor. So when it appears that it's a ballsy, gutsy risk, there is in reality the fact that it was pretty well wired to start with. And that goes back to this ability to stand there and say no. That's the whole thing — YES or NO.

"I learned as a teenager that the timing of a decision, the environment I was in — whether I wanted a piece of pie or date with Susie to the dance — remanded me to make instantaneous yes/no decisions. Or the pie would be gone or Susie would already have a date. So the stakes were so scarce and fragile that there was no room for contemplation. I had to develop an instant, almost reactive, decision. Contemplation on the scene didn't work, because by the time I'd finished a 30-second contemplation, the opportunity was gone. I learned to do all my contemplating before the fact, to sit down and do creative thinking so I knew where I stood as to any possible eventuality. Then, when it came, I was already prepared."

This was extraordinary information to me. I had lived a life, not of contemplation, but of reaction. I was the end morsel of the causal food chain, where as Bob had played out all the moves in advance. No wonder he seemed to have the edge.

He continued, "I learned that the same thing applies in selling. What kills a lot of salesmen is the willingness to take 'maybe.' The sale is there, but they prefer a gentlemanly 'Let me think it over and we'll talk next week' to a 'no.' Sure, they would prefer a 'yes.' That's in first place. 'Let me think it over and I'll call you next week' is in second place, and 'no' is a distant third, because they think they are burning their bridges.

"I disagree with that concept completely! In a selling situation, I would never, ever take a 'maybe.' Never. It's either 'yes' or 'no.' A 'maybe' is a distant third to a 'no.' A 'no' is a perfectly acceptable answer. It frees my time and my energy. Everybody's going to get nos. Maybes pile up and pretty soon I have got a briefcase full of proposals stinking up the joint.

"Now some so-called sales experts will advise you: That's too risky. You should take 'maybe.' Settle back, be more patient, let the thing mature, you'll find you'll get more in the long run. This presumes that I have asked for the order before it is time to ask for the order. You've probably heard the story about the lawyer who was embarrassed in the courtroom because he didn't know the answer to a question he had asked. That's a cardinal rule of courtroom interrogation: Don't be surprised. The same goes for this strategy. If you have gone through your sales presentation, if you have covered all the bases and read the tell-tale signs, you should already know the answer.

"So the thing that makes what I am saying — take yes or no, not maybe — not a risk proposition is that you don't ever lay it on the table until it's time to lay it on the table. If there is any little dangling participle, you're not ready. The rules of engagement are: The prospect knows going into the meeting that this is a decision-making session. All the foreplay is completed. We are either going to do the deal or go home. Everybody knows that. No surprises. Rule two: All the dangling participles are snipped off. All the details have been discussed. Then you use as your clincher, the old thing of paper-scissors-rock. In any situation, ego and fact are always counterbalanced against each other. But ego will always beat fact, just as paper always covers rock. You can NEVER lose if you have both fact and ego on your side. But you have to have ego.

"Scotty, let's talk some more about deal making. This may be real esoteric to you today, but someday it'll make more sense."

I didn't know what esoteric meant, but to this point everything else Bob had told me seemed valuable.

"The sales process is really pretty simple. The first and most important element is desire to buy, which is really tied into ego like we were just talking about. The other component is vital but less important than the first and that is need. Scotty, most of the things people buy are not bought out of need, but because of ego or desire. Yet need is nevertheless a strong motivator.

"Given that, the real name of the game is who to buy from. And most products are sold by lots of different people, so the customer has lots of choices from whom to buy. I want the customer to do business with ME. I know he likes to be with people he likes to be with. Let's say I'm trying to sell him life insurance. I don't want to talk about life insurance myself. I'd like him to talk about life insurance and why he wants to buy it. It doesn't make any difference why I think he ought to buy it — it's not my money. I'm not going to make the decision. I want to know why he would want to buy some life insurance from anybody. It could be that he just thinks it would look silly if he doesn't own any. He could have this fear that if he dies, he'll leave his wife penniless. That's rare because no one likes to think about dying. His reason for buying is usually pretty self-centered; his ego is involved. Once I know why he wants to buy, then I reinforce why he should buy it for that reason. Then the best thing in selling is always the close. I call the hand. I'm willing to take a no or a yes. So I say, let's say his name is Joe, 'Joe, have we covered everything? I really think this plan addresses your goals and objectives. From my perspective I believe we have crafted a great solution tailored to your requirements. Do we need to run through the major provisions of the plan? I'm happy to do that, but I know you're very busy and may not want a recitation of all the fine print. Naturally, I vote yes. Are you ready to wrap this up so I can let you get back to your business?'

"If I could say what is really behind all of that, it would go something like this: 'I think we've covered everything. Any questions?' Then I'd think: 'I don't know about you, but I don't have the time and I know you don't have the time. You're busier than I am and we're doing what I do. I could potentially profit from what we are doing here but we aren't doing what you do. You make widgets and right now you're not making widgets. We ought to make a decision. Frankly, the decision might be yes and it might be no. That's not for me to say. All I know is, I've said what I want to say, you've said what you want to say. We're both decision makers. Let's make a decision. I vote yes.' And before he answers me, I'd like to say, 'Gotta give you a ground rule. You won't like this, but you'll appreciate it. Your answer is not going to be "maybe, I want to sleep on it." That's an insult to you and me. It's a waste of time. So your answer has to be yes or no, or you'll lose me. I don't have time and I'm not going to allow you to have time or not to exercise the courage to make a decision. That said, what do you say?' Now I have found that happens most of the time because I got his ego involved. If he says no, he is a non-decisive wimp and he knows it. So he says what the hell, let's do it.

"Every time ego and fact come into conflict, ego is going to win. You are not going to diminish your ego. I've never seen anybody do it. Ever. Of all the tools we have as salesmen, as husbands, as friends, the strongest thing we have is ego.

"Scotty, what I am talking about is not high pressure, one-call closing. There are always some preliminaries to all this. Most of the people I do business with know me or my reputation. For the most part, these deals are wired or mostly wired. I can't afford to spend time on futile efforts."

"Mr. O'Brien, don't these 'maybes' fill up your bucket?"

"Damn, son, you're about ready to graduate from Bob's Bromides! That is exactly what I am talking about. When your bucket is full, you are stymied. You can't take advantage of opportunities, but more importantly, you're so busy trying to convert the maybes you don't even SEE the other possibilities. Be a pipe, Scotty. Be a pipe not a bucket."

As usual, my responsibilities as caddie had been handled by my auto-pilot. I was much more tuned into the most important function of the day: student. And it had been an incredible day from that standpoint. Now on the golf side of the ledger, Bob continued to have a great day. Somewhere along the way he had muttered something about 3 over par. I took that to mean 75, his career best at National, if we assume par on number 4. He made the turn at 1 under and had 3 bogeys, 2 birdies and the rest pars as we teed off on 18. Anything but a triple bogey would give him a new personal best.

I was about to see a demonstration of "winners win." To Bob, this thing was wired. He wasn't going to choke now. Tee ball. Driver straight down the middle. Six-iron. On the green to within 20 feet of the hole. Putt to six inches. Tap in for par. Bob had shot par, 72.

DISTANCE TO THE GREEN

AUGUST 23

Leadership - Bromides

I was already sweating when I met O'Brien on the 1st fairway. The sun had popped out early and was beating down without mercy. O'Brien handed me his clubs and wasted no time in telling me what was in store for today's sweltering walk.

"Scotty, we've talked a lot about how to get where you're going, attaining goals and wiring deals in your favor. But there's one thing that is missing from that multifaceted equation for success. It has to do with other people."

"You mean managing them or throwing black balls at them?" I asked.

O'Brien gave me a half-smile that told me my time for asking questions was later.

"Leadership, Scotty. How to lead, how to keep good people and deal with the difficult ones.

"I want to tell you a story about my son, but it applies to all the people who work for me and with whom I do business. This is where my son Rob became committed to me business-wise and had a different perspective of me as his leader. It is an example of one of my bromides in action. I have several bromides about leadership and one of them is 'My Ol' Man Can Whip Your Ol' Man.'

"Rob was just starting out in the insurance business. One of the places I put him when he first began, was selling insurance to employees at City Bank. I'd set up a payroll deduction system.

There was an assistant human resources guy who didn't like insurance salesmen in general, and he didn't like me in particular because I had put this program in around him. He especially resented Rob having the run of the place to sell to his employees — he was Rob's age. So he was waiting in the bushes.

"Rob sold a policy and about two months later the buyer wanted to stop the policy and get his money back. Well, this was a life insurance policy he'd bought — you don't get your money back. He didn't die, it was a risk. So he went to this HR guy and said, 'Rob O'Brien told me I could quit anytime I wanted to and get my money back because this is a savings plan. Now I can't.' They both knew that was ridiculous. But when Rob showed up the next morning, the HR guy was standing there and barred Rob from the door. He said, 'It's over.'

"So Rob came back to the office, and emotionally his whole world had caved in. He'd spent four days a week down there getting to know people and selling three to four policies a day. This was his cash cow. He came to my office and said, 'Dad, I really blew it.' He told me the story and I said, 'You didn't blow anything.' But he was really disturbed. I said, 'Let's go.' He said, 'Where are we going?' I said, 'We're gonna go talk to Frank Moore.' Now, Moore was the CEO of our insurance underwriter and a good friend of mine. So I called and told his secretary, Helen, to tell Frank I was on my way. I needed to see him. So we went down there and told Frank the story. I said, 'Frank, this can't be — this kid can't whip us around.' Frank said, 'Let's go.' So Frank and Rob and I went down in Frank's car and we walked into Ed Freeman Jr.'s office, president of the bank. We told Freeman the story, and Rob didn't say a word. Freeman called in the executive vice president and told him the story. He called in the Human Resources Vice President and told him the story. Then he called in this HR kid. The kid came walking in the door and there was me sitting there, Rob sitting there, Moore sitting there. There was everyone from his chairman on down. Of course, we just nailed him. He left the bank about three months later. Rob was reinstated and Rob's position in terms of 'my ol' man can whip your ol' man' was forever solidified. He couldn't see himself doing that yet, and the mere fact that I could, solidified my leadership. Not my fatherhood, but my leadership. I've done that on several occasions."

I handed O'Brien an 8-iron and tried to imagine being that poor sap who had crossed his son. Before I could get my mind around the humiliation, he went on.

"Leadership is a tricky thing. I guess in that respect it's a lot like parenting. Sometimes the things you have to do are really tough, but you have to do them for the good of the family. They are things that seem hurtful and sometimes they are hurtful, but for the greater good of your family or organization you have to do them. The power of a family or organization pulling together, united by a central vision, is unstoppable. That vision comes from the top and it sometimes has to be cruelly unswerving in its devotion to its guiding principles.

"Let me give you another example of a situation that caused me to do something that I wished that I hadn't had to do, but to do otherwise would have sent a compromising and unacceptable message to the others.

"At our company we have had a tradition of one big sales contest each year and afterwards we have a big party. The winners eat steak and the losers eat beans — one of those. And we always had skits. It has always been a rather prudish environment where there was no sexual innuendo. No hanky-panky. Zero.

"Traditionally, most of the young women in our firm have come from families I've known. But unnoticed by us, we were getting bigger and getting bigger quicker than we were acknowledging. No longer a little tight-knit group. So this young kid, an MBA, put on a skit that bordered on raunchy. That was embarrassing. During the skit I was consulted and I said not to stop it, we would deal with him later. After the party was over, he made a couple of comments to one of the young women. This guy was married, by the way, and spouses weren't at this luncheon. One of my vice presidents, Sharon, said to him, 'Jake, that isn't appropriate.' He said, 'I'm sorry.' But pretty soon he did it again, just as the party is breaking up. The next morning I called two witnesses to my office along with Jake. I said, 'Jake, when you walked in that door, you worked here. Right now, you do not. Don't say a word because this interview isn't gonna last 30 more seconds. Number one, you're fired. Number two, I want your key right now. Number three, Patrick is gonna walk back to your desk with you and pack up your things in this box. Then he'll walk you to your car. I don't ever want to see you again or hear from you. Don't call me. Don't write me. If you even think about causing me any trouble over this incident, I flat guarantee that you will be the sorriest kid that ever walked the streets of Kansas City. Now get out of my office.' Now that story spread in about 20 minutes. The whole company knew — don't mess with the old man. You can go so far, but you go one step over that line and it's over. It's over — there is no messing around."

He paused as I watched him sink a three-foot putt. I wiped my forehead off with an already damp towel.

"But he knew he was in the wrong. You'd warned him?" I asked.

"Oh, yes. He knew. There was no vagueness in what he was saying. It was vulgar. Everyone had been subjected to it. They were waiting for me to drop the ball on him. In order to be a leader, people have got to see you in that light."

"Mr. O'Brien, how have you handled that stuff with the women in your office? Have you ever had a problem?"

"Good question, Scotty. The male/female situation is something every professional has to learn to handle. In the sense that I believe you have to stroke the egos of people who work for and with you, you have to be careful not to cross certain lines and to learn where those barriers are early on.

"Back when I first started my business, I really built up my secretary's ego. Probably because I was young (not much older than she was), I built the fire a little strong. I don't mean in a sexual way, just too personal. Not enough space between us. She got the idea that we had something besides her being just my secretary. So her transgression was to pass it on to some other people that she and I had a thing going. Now she didn't say it was physical, which, in fact, it was far from. We never had any contact — nothing.

"There was a day when I was going across the street to a drug store to get a sandwich. I said, 'Ellen, you want to go with me?' No big deal. We had lunch together. So she began to use that — she'd drop it, 'When I was having lunch with Bob yesterday...' to some other young girl in the office. So that's when I had to call her in and say, 'You and I know that's not accurate.' She said, 'I didn't mean that.' She was an Oklahoma farm girl — but I knew she really understood the significance, the impact on me. So I called in the office manager. The office manager was a lady about six feet tall who ran the financial office. They called me a general agent. On paper she worked for me but in reality, not a chance. She'd seen young sales managers like me come and go 15 times. I also called Ellen into the office, closed the door and told Mrs. Jones what was going on and she understood. Ellen started crying, and she quit. That was the first time I learned that it can be overdone. When you reprimand or when you stroke egos, there's real skill and risk involved.

"There was another incident, and it was the only time I remember having to pull someone back to where we needed to be. I hired this saleswoman named Dora seven or eight years ago. She was good. I had done a good job of molding her — she was my person. I was her father figure. So one day we had this female group rep from one of the companies selling their products. Those two were in this tiff and they got me in it. Scotty, always defend your people in front of an adversary whether they're right or wrong. Well, I took Dora's side and I told off this group rep — I just sliced and diced her. She left crying. I said what I needed to say to prove to Dora that I was her leader.

"But a week later, Dora misinterpreted what I'd done. She thought she had more than a professional relationship, that we had a special thing. No matter what she did, she assumed she was impervious to harm. She couldn't walk in harm's way. So she pulled some shenanigan inside the office. I called her into my office and read her the riot act. For a while, it confused her. I said, 'Now, Dora, when Molly did this, she was an outsider. I don't care if you were right or wrong, I'm gonna go to the wall for you. When you're doing it in the family, you'd better be right. But you're not right. You're using what you think is a privileged relationship with me to get away with something that isn't right. It doesn't work, Dora, don't ever do it again.' I said, 'I know you'll figure this out intellectually or you'll leave. Either way is okay, Dora. If you can't figure it out, I don't want you in with me.' It took her about a week. She figured it out and said, 'Mr. O'Brien, you are really right.'"

O'Brien ripped a 1-iron, low into the prevailing breeze on 3 that landed him smack in the middle of the fairway.

"Nice one," I commented, taking the club back. "Have you ever had to fire someone you didn't want to?"

"Not exactly, but one time I fired everyone," he answered.

"Everyone?" I laughed. Somehow, I knew this would be a good yarn.

"Scotty, when you start a sales organization from dead scratch, it's incumbent that the very first person whom you recruit be absolutely the highest quality that you're capable of recruiting because everything will be built from that base. If you compromise in order to get someone on board and he's not high caliber, he's the best you'll ever get. You can't recruit above that guy. I hadn't learned that yet. So I had two B-minus kind of guys and seven studs. Young studs, some of whom were pretty aggressive. Probably could have been winners. But they were watching the B-minuses. I didn't really have control of them after a while because of the two B-minuses.

"So they formed a junior executive committee, came in my office and wanted to see me. All seven came in. This was the Friday afternoon before Christmas. They said, 'We have formed a junior executive committee.' I said, 'Oh, is that like a union?' They said, 'Well, we don't call it a union, but we'd like to negotiate for next year.' They wanted to talk office allocations, financial allocation and such. I said, 'Okay, I'll tell you what we're gonna do. The first thing you need to do is decide what you're gonna call your agency.' They said, 'What do you mean?' I said, 'You guys don't work here anymore.' This is an honest-to-God true story. They said, 'What are you talking about?' I said, 'All seven of you are fired. I don't do mutiny.'"

O'Brien chuckled at his own memory of the moment. "All of a sudden, they were babbling idiots. I said, 'You've come in here, and this is mutiny. I don't care if you say you were just kidding. You're capable of being mutineers and I don't want any mutineers around. You're outta here.' So to answer your question, that took my agency from nine people to two people, both of whom were losers and there was some hint of despair in terms of wondering where we were gonna go from there. You have a pretty sick feeling in the pit of your stomach. But what you have to do is learn and start over. So I hired a high caliber guy and life went on."

He missed an uphill putt. The ball stopped short of the cup and rolled back past his feet. He just rolled his head, cracking his neck, and took another whack at it with what I thought would be too much force. It circled quickly around the cup once and went in.

Out of his pocket, he took out a square sheet of paper, unfolded it and handed it to me.

"This is what I give to my managers and people I'm trying to fine-tune when it comes to leadership."

I wiped my hands of sweat and took the paper. It said "Bob's Bromides: Essentials of Leadership." He gave me time to read it as we stamped on to the next hole.

It said:

1. Ego Enhancement
2. Father Figure
3. My Ol' Man Can Whip Your Ol' Man
4. Fearless
5. Making the Team
6. Insiders
7. Problem Solver
8. Straw Boss
9. Guiding Light

He looked at me when I'd finished and I knew this was my time to ask the questions.

"Mr. O'Brien, I don't know where to start. These topics are intriguing just by their titles."

"Well, why not start at the top?"

"Gee, I wish George were here. He'd love this stuff and I can never repeat within 10 percent the meaning or the cleverness that you have."

"Well, where is he?"

"I think he had Colonel Tower. You know the fellow who was a politician in Kentucky? Wears the white suits all the time? We won't see George until late. The Colonel likes to tell all his stories every time out."

"Scotty, my wife has got us booked for some black-tie thing at the club tonight. Jeez, I hate those deals. What are you and George doing tonight?"

"Well, I guess we were going to do what we usually do on Thursday night. And Friday night. And Saturday night. Like we do every night — eat at the caddyshack and head for NuWay."

"What's NuWay? Is that some pyramid scheme?"

"Oh, no. That's the Drive-In down on Troost, just north of the A & P. Great milk shakes and onion rings. The best pie anywhere. And it's George's and my think tank. We have solved most of life's great philosophical mysteries down there this summer."

"Man, that sounds great. Let's see...NuWay versus the black-tie deal. No contest. I'm with you, Scotty. My wife is really going to hate me for this, but I think I deserve a night out with the boys. Could you and George stand an old geezer like me?"

"We would be honored to show you the sublimity of a great O-ring and Cherry Coke. What time should we meet you?"

"What's your regular time? Eight?"

"Sounds great. We'll see you there."

I was waiting patiently in the caddyshack when George arrived from his marathon with Colonel Tower. From the look on his face, it had been brutal.

"Scotty, that blowhard just wears me out. For at least the 10th time this summer I heard about his bet on Man O' War, mint juleps with J. Edgar Hoover, his parties with Adolph Rupp and his affair with one of the actresses in the Wizard of Oz. I didn't ask him if it was one of the Munchkins."

"George, I invited Bob O'Brien to join us at NuWay."

"Why would you do that? So he could laugh at you?"

"No, no. We're meeting him at eight."

"Did you tell him to bring plenty of cash? He's probably not used to dining at such highfalutin' places. Wait a minute. I almost forgot. You always stiff him anyway, so I guess you'll be pickin' up the check. Scotty, do you realize how much tip money you have walked away from this summer?"

"Yeah, yeah. Well, it's been worth it, George. While you were hearing about some deviant behavior of Colonel Tower and a Munchkin, I was getting a valuable lesson in leadership, which Bob has kindly agreed to continue for your benefit tonight."

"Okay, Scotty, let me shower and we're outta here."

You can imagine the number of Jaguar sedans that pulled up at NuWay that summer. I'm sure that was a first for Big Dog, the owner and chief hamburger flipper at NuWay. When Bob pulled up, Big Dog actually changed aprons, two days ahead of schedule.

George and I had arrived earlier to make sure Bob didn't beat us there. Of course, we ensconced ourselves in our usual booth. Mary Beth, the veteran waitress at NuWay, usually discouraged customers from sitting there until eight. If George and I didn't show by then, she released it to the general public. She also lived by the universal monetary system of tipping, so some of our geetus wound up in her apron and she thereby preserved our home away from home.

I was struck instantly by the great contrast of Bob's entry into NuWay and that of the typical customer. Now Bob is not an immodest or pompous character, really just the opposite. But class and confidence are indelible and transcend. I don't know if Bob was born a leader or became one, but when he walked through the door there was no doubt that he was a person who knew what he was all about. It reminded me immediately of Jorgen and the mirror phenomenon. Like I said, it hit home immediately and it made me think that that was how I wanted people to think of me.

He warmly greeted George and me as equals and as fraternity brothers of the drive-in world. He was as at ease in that grease-slickened booth as he was in the boardroom of a Fortune 500 company.

"Whatcha having, boys?"

Now George and I were health food junkies back in those days. My favorite was a double thick chocolate milk shake with a big piece of apple pie, while George was a Cherry Coke and onion ring aficionado. Bob got right with it and ordered up a cup of Big Dog's java and some lemon pie.

"So this is what I've been missing by dining at National. Fellas, this reminds me of a place of my youth. I won't regale you with how I misspent that youth, but suffice it to say we walked a very thin line between law-abiding and mischievous. It is a subtle and often mysterious force that pushes us to one side of that line for good. I somehow turned out to be a fairly prosperous and legitimate business person, but fate could have cast me in some other direction. Maybe that's why I'm here tonight. I see two very promising souls who might benefit from some of the things I learned the hard way. I didn't have a mentor but if I had, it sure would have saved me a lot of heartache. Now, Scotty, where were we when we broke up this afternoon?"

I pulled the sheet of paper he had given me on the golf course out of my shirt pocket, uncreased it and smoothed it out on the Formica table. It stuck. But everything and everybody stuck to

NuWay. Item number one on the list was Ego Enhancement.

"Scotty, you recall how ego worked to my advantage in a couple of instances? Remember when I flipped that guy for $400,000?" George's head popped right up. "George, I didn't physically flip the guy. We had a coin toss and that settled a little difference of opinion on some contract language. We also talked about how ego works in selling situations and how when ego and fact collide, ego wins. However, in leadership, ego enhancement is a little different. Ego enhancement is like an emotional currency that you pay your people with — constantly. Those whom you would lead must have their ego enhanced each and every time they encounter you or when they hear you've said something about them. Never, ever forget that anytime you say something about someone — negative or positive — you should assume that it is going to get back to him. When what you have said that is positive comes back around, it is golden and magnified. For some people it has even greater impact than if you had told them directly.

"But this is not ego stroking. The idea is that you have enhanced your position with your people by paying them with this emotional currency. You have earned the right to correct or reprimand them should that be required. It is not a phony build up, but you are positioning yourself to say what has to be said, however tough it is, whenever the occasion demands. If you haven't built that relationship through ego enhancement, not stroking, you don't have the right to be tough and it will backfire on you."

"George," I said, "you know that's right. When someone respects you or cares about you, his criticism is helpful not hurtful. That's why I'm here this summer, I guess. If I didn't believe Coach Robbie cared about me, I wouldn't be here. I'd have just told him to get lost. What's the next one?"

"The next leadership topic I call Father Figure. When I was

younger, in my 30s, I didn't really understand this one and it hurt me. As we built our organization and started to take on more people, some of them were my age, some were younger and several older. When that happens there is a tendency to want to be their brother or friend, and it's really hard to be the father. Until I recognized the leader needs to be the father, I wasn't the leader I could be. I don't know if this had something to do with the relationship I had with my father, but ultimately I came to realize that most people are looking for this type of leader. A strong defender. A non-judgmental defender. You know how a father is: Right or wrong, these are my kids and by golly I'm going to defend them. Man, that is some powerful leader whose people think he is their father figure. It's like blood — very thick and very dedicated.

"If you nurture this environment, if they belong with you to begin with, your people will do anything not to disappoint you and they will be there through thick and thin. These days most corporations cannot foster this feeling. They are not loyal to their people and when the going gets tough, each tries to see who can cut and run the quickest. The corporations trim their payrolls and release those who used to be loyal employees and now the employees are just as quick to look for greener pastures. Who can blame them? There's no father figure to protect them.

"Also remember that when the father must discipline, he should have the sensitivity to know that a reprimand should be done privately. Don't ever show up your children in front of their peers and don't do the same to your employees. It is a sin that they will be very slow to forgive."

"Mr. O'Brien..."

"Call me Bob, guys."

"Bob, what about that fella Jake you fired?"

"Good call, Scotty. I had to disown him by firing him. He did not see me as a father figure or he would not have demonstrated such a dishonorable trait in front of me. When I chose not to have him as a member of our family, I also gave up the requirement to treat him as one of us. I hated to do that, but it would have been far worse if I had tolerated it. Couldn't do it. I try not to be harsh, and there are many times I have to take people aside for criticism and advice. But I have earned the right to do that. Many, and perhaps most organizations don't have that luxury. So what do they do? They live with it which just kills morale and productivity. We fix it and fix it right now. That's a huge edge that we have always had. The ability to go to our people and engage them in a dialogue that helps us and helps them."

"Bob, does this relate to next one on the list, My Ol' Man Can Whip Your Ol' Man?" George asked.

"George, it's part of the same piece but it takes it to little higher plane. Let me explain.

Scotty, remember the story with Rob's human resources guy or inside with someone like Jake? That's part of the picture. What I'm talking about here is courage. Guts. I hope as a small boy, you had the feeling that your dad could protect you from anything out there. It made you feel safe and secure. It gave you the security to develop and grow outside of a fearful environment. You just don't know how important that it is. It supercharges your maturation. And it makes you strong and not mean or petty. What happens to a puppy that is mistreated? Makes it into a cur.

"The same environment has to be supplied by the leader so that his people can develop and everyone prospers. The courage of the leader begets courage by the team. Man, you see it in sports all the time. One guy steps up and says we're going win, we're going to beat these guys. That's courage and when everyone believes it, great things occur.

"So how does the leader develop this feeling in his people? It ain't by lip service, guys. You have to go out there and do it. Remember what I told you about successful people — they have the willingness to do what others will not. That is the essence of leadership and that's why they pay the big bucks for that talent.

"There is one more element of this that shows up on the list as Number 4: Fearless. Guys, if they see the leader whipped, the game is over, the jig is up. They must never see you defeated mentally or physically or emotionally. Way before your time we had a President who had polio. He led the nation through the darkest economic times and a World War. But you know, most people didn't even know that he was crippled. To them he was fearless. Roosevelt had an amazing counterpart in Britain, Churchill. People laid down their lives to follow these men. If you are going to lead, then you have to accept that with it goes the responsibility of tirelessness and courage. This trait comes up huge in times of crisis and confusion. That's when a decisive and action-oriented leader must be in place. It's easy to be fearless when everything is going well. That's not fearless, that's self-indulgence. It's really hard when you and your gang have been thrown a major league black ball. The average guy will hunker down when things get tough. It's this bunker mentality that is really destructive. You can't believe the amount of energy wasted on trying to preserve the status quo, rather than taking the initiative to adapt and create and get ahead of the curve — not be buried behind it. The courageous leader will strike out in new directions to survive. Remember the gang is going to be watching you to see how you react. Stand tall."

"Bob, I think I can relate to this expression, Making the Team, but what does it mean to you?"

"Well, what do you think it means, Scotty?"

"I think it means that everybody wants to associate with a winning team. They want to make the team so they can be on that winner."

"Very, very insightful. See, what the leader really wants to create is the feeling that his team wants to be with him. It's like the boy who is really proud to be with his dad. Man, what a powerful motivator that is as a parent. We would do anything to make our kids proud of us and doing everything to keep them from being ashamed of us. We all would love to be our kids' hero.

"Same with the leader. The true leader creates an atmosphere, an aroma that is so attractive that it can't be resisted. Did you guys ever read the story about the sirens that supposedly lived off the shore of Sicily? Their song was so beautiful that the sailors had to steer their boats toward them even though it meant sure destruction on the rocky shoreline. Now that is compelling. Well, the true leader can create an atmosphere that compels others to join his team, and once on the team to believe that they are exactly where they should be. The Marine Corps has it: Semper Fi. The leader makes it worthy to be on that team. That kind of cohesion and esprit de corps is unbeatable."

"Bob, what do you mean by Number six: Insiders?"

"George, that's a subtle one compared to the others but really valuable. We have been talking about the sort of bombastic methods of leadership: fearlessness, courage, father figure. 'Insiders' is much quieter but equally powerful in establishing leadership. I guess it's somewhat akin to what happens in Congress. The deals are all wired behind the scene in the cloakrooms and hallways, then they go in and give their speeches and take the vote. To the outsider, it looks like the speeches and the voting are the real thing, but the fact is that the deals are wired before the gavel is struck.

"Too subtle for you? Let me put it this way, a good leader works behind the scenes in private to make sure that he has brought everyone into his confidence. This is best done privately and singularly. Some leadership techniques are for the masses, but some of the most powerful are delivered individually. How do I do that? Easy. I walk around and talk to people. I want to know what's on their minds and I want them to know what's on mine."

"Bob, Problem Solver is one of the few on the list that seem obvious on the surface."

"George, that one is pretty straightforward. But there is a little twist to it that I'd like you to remember when you are running a big multinational corporation."

George puffed up with that comment. Bob was doing some ego thing that George, of course, missed because he was the object of the O'Brien charm.

"Some cultures have had what they called oracles. Usually the oracle was off in some remote location. I always picture the oracle up in some cave, high on a mountain top. Anyway, when the people had a difficult problem to solve they would take it to the oracle. Sometimes they had to bring a gift or sacrifice for the oracle to do his thing, but the oracle would go into his trance or incantation, which was his problem solving mode. Because of the price you had to pay to get this wisdom, you didn't bring just any everyday problem — you brought the oracle the tough ones. Same with the leader. The leader shouldn't want to solve all the problems. That's too much management and not enough delegation. The leader should give as much responsibility and authority as he possibly can to his gang. Responsibility without authority is hollow and frustrating for everyone.

"So the leader must function as the problem solver of last resort. His analytics, his strategies must be super-credible. Now for the twist: Not every leader has this capacity. This analytical ability falls into the realm of intellect and creativity. A great leader can fall short here and still be a leader. On the other aspects- no way. He must have them because they have to do with the connection a leader makes with the soul of his people. That can't be replaced. However you can have a member of your 'army' help you with the analytics. This problem solver might not be a very good leader. But if he thinks he is or should be, you'll trade ego for his skills. Give him a high rank and leverage his strengths. In a large organization, this is the value of financial people or legal people or the actuary. In a small organization there is the trusted sidekick — Tonto to the Lone Ranger.

"The next one on my list reminds me of one of my first sales managers, the Straw Boss. Actually it reminds me of just the opposite point I want to make. This guy was not a salesman. Had he been a good salesman, he wouldn't have been able to afford to take the job as sales manager. Good salespeople within the company made much more than this guy. Now he was a good recruiter and that might have been his saving grace, but to us he was an empty suit. A big hat with no cattle. But he was forever setting goals for us that we knew he couldn't have made in a million years. We had absolutely no respect for the guy. A leader cannot afford that disrespect. The rule is, don't ask your gang to do something that you won't or can't do yourself. You might have to send someone off for some grungy work, but make sure you did it one time yourself. Another thing a leader avoids is sending one of his troops off to do something that is beyond his scope. It is unfair to set someone up for failure. Is it okay to ask someone to 'stretch?' Sure, that's how we grow, but if you do that, provide a safety net so he doesn't get wiped out or fearful the next time he tries to stretch."

"Now, what is 'Guiding Light?' Sounds almost religious," I said.

"Well, for your people it almost will be. In a great organization it becomes a matter of faith. They will know in their bones that they are on the path to success if they ride with you. It has to do with following through and helping your people reach their own goals. Again, if you can't do that, they won't stay with you. You'll just be building someone else's organization. It has to be obvious to them that by staying with you, they will accomplish whatever they want and you will not abandon them."

NuWay probably had not been home to such a management seminar before or since.

It was a lot to absorb in one evening. My brain was on overload, combining these new revelations with everything else O'Brien and the others had tried to teach me. I was secretly glad he'd given me the paper, so I could sit down later with George and not have to struggle to remember each point.

In the years since, I have learned that these essential bromides — like the steps to goal attainment — are indeed essential and indispensable in establishing a rapport with people and becoming a leader. Sacrifice just one and all can be lost. I have combined them with Jorgen's mirror image philosophy, and I've gotten where I wanted to go.

I have retyped and recopied "Bob's Bromides" many times over as I shared his secrets with select people over the years. But I still keep the original he gave me in a zippered pocket of my golf bag.

DISTANCE to the GREEN

LAST DAY

The Secret Driver

I had specifically asked Richard Nelson to make sure that I had at least one more opportunity to carry Bob O'Brien's bag before I had to head back to school. For the past week I had given Richard a day-by-day countdown for my departure, reminding him that I only had six days or five days left before I was to leave. I was struck by the huge difference in my attitude from that first day. I vividly recalled my pain at being banished to the caddyshack by Coach Robbie. Now I was actually feeling a different pain or fear. The fear was that I was going to leave this great place never to return and that I might leave without asking Bob some questions that I just knew were going to open up the remaining secrets of his success. I had a feeling that I had the main ingredients already, but I wanted to ask him a few questions about a coarser subject: money and wealth and success. I guess I felt comfortable enough to ask him about those things. Everybody knows those are questions that a polite person doesn't ask, but I didn't think I was going to have many chances to find these things out from the boys back at school.

So when I saw Rich the day before I was planning to leave and pointed my index finger at him indicating my last day, I was relieved when he smiled and said, "Grab his bag, Scotty, he's waiting for you on the putting green."

As always, Bob, had a big smile and a hearty greeting. As we shook hands, he remarked, "Well, Scotty, it's about time for you to return to the ivy-covered walls, isn't it?"

"Yes, Mr. O'Brien, the Athens of the Plains is calling me home. I'll be heading out in the morning. I was afraid that I wasn't going to see you before I left."

"No way, Scotty. We still have some ground to cover. I was thinking about our last meeting, and we got to talking about wiring deals and such and as I thought about that, I guess I figured that probably sounded pretty mercenary to a young idealist like you. I think a good topic today might be why deals are important and why the outcome of the deals — money — is important and how you handle all of that."

The guy was amazing! How he could always be two steps ahead of me was uncanny. "Mr. O'Brien, I am really interested in just that, but I had no idea how to express it or even if I could express it. I just know that a guy like me sees a person like you, wealthy and successful, and wonders how you do that. How do I get to that place?"

"Well, first, Scotty, my goal when I started was not necessarily to make all the money in the world. I knew what I didn't want, but, like you, I wasn't really sure how to avoid that place either. I have been blessed but the things I have already shared with you are the guiding principles to success, goal attainment being so essential. But as we play today let's talk about success and what goes along with that. It's a beautiful day for a stroll."

And it was a magnificent day. Usually at that time of year the dew point was so high that the morning golfers' shoes got very wet even walking the 1st hole. But that day it was fairly dry with a gentle breeze out of the southeast. A few contrails streaked an otherwise cloudless sky.

"Scotty, I think you will remember one of my tenets of success is that successful people are willing to do what others are unwilling to do. I recall that one of my first business goals was to accomplish $1,000,000 in sales for my company during my first year. That was a feat that no other salesman had ever done in his first year. So I deployed what is called 'The Pay Yourself First/$10 per Month' savings plan. Now the details of the plan are not as important as your knowing that I got very, very good at this presentation. I had this talk down cold and because I had it rote, I abhorred giving it. Hated giving it! It was like standing under a basketball goal and not moving and shooting little bank shots all day. How long can you do that? An hour? Well, this was like doing that eight hours a day, every day. It required every bit of self-discipline to continue to do that. I could have easily tricked it up, or worse, I could have started to slough off, do it sloppily and carelessly or leave parts out of it. But I didn't. So by developing a process that was highly successful and religiously sticking to that process, I was able to achieve my goal. But it required great self-discipline to give that sales presentation over and over and over.

"Now hear me on this. I practiced the essentials of goal achievement to the letter and a part of that process was something that really wasn't pleasant to me, cold calling and giving a presentation by rote. My goal was easy to see: First person in the history of the company to achieve $1,000,000 in sales in his rookie year. Did it pass the smell test? Darn right it did. What was the path? The path was the 'Pay Yourself First' spiel done as many times as was required to give me a mathematical certainty at my goal. And I broke it down to the hour. But as it relates to the formula for success — doing what others wouldn't do — I knew where the void was. The void was the ability to tirelessly prospect, schedule appointments and deliver my talk with conviction. The fourth part of goal achievement is commitment, and Scotty, this was my first big test where I could keep score with dollars and I was committed to my very soul.

"One night, Mary Jo and I had her parents over for dinner. I had scheduled some calls for later that evening. Right before dinner one of my appointments called and canceled. Well, that threw me into a near anxiety attack. This cancellation was destroying my plan and creating tremendous pressure. So while dinner was going on, I went in another room, picked up the phone book and began cold calling until I replaced that appointment. That is commitment. Lastly, did I pass go? I sure did, and I also passed the finish line with my goal accomplished.

"Now there are people who fancy themselves as 'sales people' who have a little success and convince themselves that what they are doing is difficult and therefore they ultimately should be successful. They are delusional. There is a another type of salesperson who exists in a fantasy world, the weird duck who likes cold-calling. I mean, there are people who happen to like this part of the process. However they aren't disciplining themselves to do something they don't like. It is a fetish at work. Scotty, what I am talking about is the sustaining knowledge which a successful person carries inside: that he or she is capable and willing to do something others can't. It's the competitive edge that tells you that you will succeed because you have in the past and you will in future because you are willing to PAY THE PRICE. Whatever that requires. If you set your goal, see your path and commit, you know that you won't be denied because you WILL do whatever it takes to see it through. It is an essential ingredient of successful people."

"Mr. O'Brien, how do you know when you've got that ingredient?"

"Well, Scotty, I can't just bestow it on you. You have to have the right core values, you have to have the right stuff, but it must be tempered by experience. Test yourself. Set a goal and do what is required to accomplish it. Set a higher goal, then pay that price. Then set a higher goal and accept that challenge. Then you'll know. Along the way you'll take a few shots, get the stuffing knocked out of you. If you can rebound and reach your goal, then you'll know."

"Mr. O'Brien, are those the type of people who work for you?"

"Many are. I have been very fortunate in that regard. When they come to us they usually are not fully formed. But it becomes apparent very quickly which of them has that rare ability to do what others are unwilling to do. One of the things we look for in our people or try to teach our people is that concept you and I have talked about: Covering Homebase. Actually Scotty, I have used Covering Homebase in a couple of ways. Both meanings are critical aspects of success. Your functional homebase is your ground, your current meal ticket. It has to be covered to survive and move forward. I know that sounds vague but that's because it is so universal. Your moral homebase has to be covered. Your personal financial homebase has to be covered. Your business homebase has to be covered or you can't progress from there.

"This is especially valuable to our people when it comes to personal financial management. There's nothing in my mind more tenuous than a company whose leaders make a lot of money but are essentially broke. They are always running scared. Others might say that's good because it keeps them working harder. Wrong. It eats at them and gives them ulcers and heart attacks. They make bad decisions and that hurts all of us.

"As I've indicated, homebase doesn't just have to do with money. Instead, it is the absolute necessity of establishing courses of action to keep body and soul together in terms of functioning. For instance, in business it means you get one thing going for you and you keep it going before moving on to another venture. You never let the first thing die because it is your business homebase and you can't let that go until another homebase is firm. It is the essence of bridge building. You sink a pier. Make it secure, then move on to the next, make it secure, move on to the next, and so on. Anything different is lily padding, and you better move fast because that lily pad is going down if you stay too long.

"Covering homebase has its most dire circumstances in our personal financial life. Let me tell you a story that brought all this home to me very vividly. There was this guy named O'Neill from St. Louis. Tim O'Neill was the 'top dog' salesman of my original company. I was going to a convention in Florida where he was going. I called his secretary and found out the flight he was going to be on coming back from Miami to St. Louis. I booked myself on that flight and when I made my reservation I told them I was traveling with Mr. O'Neill and wondered if the seat next to him was vacant. Yes, it was, they told me. I booked myself into the middle seat of this long flight from Miami to St. Louis. I hate the middle seat because of my long legs, but I wanted to ride back with Mr. O'Neill. Now he hardly knew who I was, but I made sure he at least knew that I was coming from the same meeting and that I was a $1,000,000 salesman and so on. Not that it would impress him, but at least it would be worth talking about. Probably. Maybe. So we got on the airplane and I said, 'Hi, I'm Bob O'Brien. First convention...' You know, blah, blah, blah. I got his ego all stirred up and everything. In effect, I got him to tell me some of his secrets of success. All salesmen have big egos and he was delighted to have me listen to him."

"Our favorite subject, right, Mr. O'Brien?"

"You bet, Scotty, our favorite subject. I wanted to know how he did all those big deals but somehow, like today, we got on the subject of finance. Money and so forth. All of a sudden I started sensing fear. I knew it was on his mind — I could just tell. He was a worried man. He was probably 55 years old then. To make a long story short, by the time we got to St. Louis, I knew I had become this guy's bucket to dump in. Turned out he was making over $150,000 a year, which was a lot of money at the time. Still is, but I was making $350 a month. I also learned he had been making that for about 10 or 15 years. I learned that his house was worth damn near $800,000. His kids all went to private schools, then on to St. Louis U. AND HE WAS BANKRUPT. Was probably going to have to declare bankruptcy. He had forgotten that it ain't how much you earn — but the difference is between that and what you spend. He hadn't done any financial management.

"He was crying by the time we got to Lambert Field in St. Louis and I'm consoling Mr. O'Neill. His wife didn't know about the trouble they were in — he'd married an upscale lady. Kids didn't know and he was alone with that fact. He owed everybody, his house was mortgaged to the hilt, and he didn't have any money. He shot himself the next week. Killed himself. That was a real blow to me. I might have even contributed. I was probably the only one he talked to and got it all out on the table. He couldn't live with it. Killed himself in the apartment above the garage, in their carriage house, with a .38 revolver.

"So, no homebase equals trouble. One of the things that has been very important to me is personal financial management. If you successfully manage your own financial affairs, you are always in a position to say no. I look back on some of my deals where I had to say no. If I had not been financially secure, if I hadn't had homebase covered, then I would have been over a barrel. I would not have had the courage not to bluff. But I was bullet proof, not frightenable.

"One of my main goals was to get my personal financial home-base covered. Then I extended that to other areas. I certainly extend it to my core business. I see guys get their core business going then they branch off and they forget the principle of selling the $10-a-month savings plan. They forget who brung them to the dance. It's the thing that gives you the bulwark.

"It applies everywhere. You don't cheat on your wife. That base is covered. You're not vulnerable to some girl calling up, 'Hi, is Bobby there?' Homebase ain't covered if that could happen. Financial, your business, the people you do business with, your employees, the caliber of the people who are your customers. Every facet of your life. If your homebase isn't covered, you're vulnerable. They can get in there and get to you.

"If you have homebase covered, you can walk away from any deal that doesn't smell right. You are bulletproof and you are not bluffing. You are not tempted. You don't need it and don't want it; otherwise you're soiled. No compromise. No compromise on money or integrity. No lily padding, because if you land on a lily pad you better hop quick or you are going down."

"Mr. O'Brien, you have obviously done very well in your business career, but you turned out a lot different from O'Neill. How come?"

"Scotty, it's funny how much time people spend on acquiring assets and how little time they spend on conserving them. I came at this from two directions. First let me tell you how I didn't do it. My good friend Jay Edwards came back from two and a half years in the Army as a private during the Korean War with $6,000 in his pocket. He is worth $15 or maybe $20 million by now, in cash. His personal financial rule is absolutely the best one. It goes like this: If you never spend any money needlessly, you can't save any more money than that. He doesn't reach into his pocket unless it's necessary. He only spends money that has to be spent. The discipline that takes is unbelievable. I can't do that. So the other way to save money — not as effective as Jay's but nevertheless a sure-fire way — is to pay yourself first. It's the same sales talk I perfected years ago. Every month I take a percentage of my income off the top and I put it away. I have done this for years, and I do it without fail. It became a habit. I took it off the top, and spent the rest. There's never anything left. But I never, ever invade my nest egg. Never, ever. Like it never existed. What's it for? A disaster, but mostly it's so I've got homebase covered. I can always say 'no way.'

"It has worked. My house is free and clear. When I built it, I paid for it. When the bricks came, I wrote a check. When the wood came, I wrote a check. When the laborers came, same deal. I never owed a nickel on the house. So I can afford to say, 'Na, I'm not gonna do it. You can't exert financial pressure on me.'"

"But Mr. O'Brien, not everybody has the money you do."

"Good point, Scotty, but they have another type of currency and that is their values. Covering homebase transcends the financial. When you sell your soul, you are bankrupt whether you ever had money or not. That is what Tim O'Neill taught me — fear when the devil comes to collect. I learned it the easy way. I learned it by finagling a seat on an airplane."

What a story! The O'Neill story hit me hard. I was struck by the intensity of it, as well as the fact that it rang so true. Sure it was dramatic, but I didn't think Bob had embellished it a bit. I was really thankful that he had shared it with me. I guess I didn't even have to con my way on to an airplane to learn that one. Each of Bob's anecdotes and bromides stimulated new questions. I started to panic. We were on the back 9 and I still felt like there was more I needed to know before the round was over. More importantly, I wanted Bob's advice on what should I do. I wanted him to pull out his crystal ball and see my future and give me the unerring advice that would chart my course. What was my path to be?

"Mr. O'Brien, I don't know how to ask this question either. Maybe you can't answer it, but I'd sure like to know what you think I should do with my future."

He chuckled. "Scotty, I'd be depriving you of all the pain, mystery and fun if I gave you that answer. But let's talk about some general parameters. First, let me say the answer is different for every person. The path I took is probably unsuitable for many, if not most people. But I think I know you well enough to give you some general advice.

"However I'd like to couch it in terms that should be familiar to you by now. Let's use the goal attainment model that we have talked about in the past. What is your goal, Scotty?"

"Well, Mr. O'Brien, I have been giving that some thought, although you'll admit it is a huge question when we are talking about one's life. I'll take a stab at it. I guess I'd like to do something like you have done. I want to be successful, happy, and prosperous."

This time he didn't chuckle. He laughed. I felt the heat of embarrassment rising up my neck. "Scotty, you and 300,000,000 others want that one. You want the American Dream and you can have it, too. It's not as easy as it used to be, but if you use goal attainment you'll be ahead of 99 percent of the others in this great country. Let me make a couple of comments before we try to define your goal a little more precisely. First, the definition of success is very different for each person. It has a lot to do with the standards you set and your vision of yourself. Secondly, happiness is most elusive. Many people believe that happiness is a birthright. It is absolutely and positively not. I don't know if we have enough time today or tomorrow or next week to figure out what happiness is, but I do know this: It is every person's personal responsibility to seek it and it comes from inside. It is not really a function of time and place. You can be happy, ecstatic even, if you are of a mind to be, no matter where you are or what your fortunes are. I have seen literally thousands of examples of that. A sickness of some generations is that they think that their country or the company they work for has the responsibility for making them happy. You have to manage that on your own. Some of my happiest times occurred when I had no money, when my life was very uncomplicated, and I was living right in the moment. Another source of incredible joy has been my kids and my grandkids. They have brought me the highest of highs in my lifetime. And your last goal, prosperity, as we have discussed, has to be handled right or you wind up like O'Neill — a broken and desperate man.

"Nevertheless, I'll try to help you interpret your remarks so we can move forward. I'm going to say that your goal is to be a player. By that I mean you want to be a captain of your own ship, you want to position yourself where there is great potential for personal and financial enrichment. Does this mean you necessarily have to have your own business? Sometimes that's the case, but let me give you an example otherwise.

"I think I have given the people who work for me that kind of opportunity. I call it owning your own ball. Owning your own ball is the best feeling that an employer can give to an employee. It is really better than money. You know why I say that? Because people will leave you no matter how much they are making if they don't feel that they are valuable and somewhat in control of their destiny."

I thought of Case and happiness = control.

"Scotty, people really don't focus on their salary except twice a month on payday. If people aren't excited about going to work, that effects them much more than how much money they make.

Now if they don't have their financial homebase covered, they are constantly tormented, but my point is that money isn't the factor. It's this feeling of owning their own ball — that they have a sphere of influence. Choose your work so that you can find that feeling. It's very fulfilling and enriching. Too bad many companies treat their people like irresponsible children. They just don't trust them."

I remembered what Jorgen had said about trust. All my lessons were looping back on one another. But time was really running out on me now. It hit me as we were walking from the 18th green. Summer was over and I was about to head back to school. I might not ever have a chance to learn from Bob O'Brien again. I had two dangling participles left (to use his phrase). First, there was no way to thank him. My stiffing him had gotten pretty lame, but he still got a kick out of it although I wasn't sure why. But a question had begun to nag me and I needed a chance to ask this big question.

"Scotty," he offered, "let's get a Coke in the grill."

I had never officially been in the Men's Grill at National, although there had been a couple of late night sorties with Richard's blessing that had yielded cheeseburgers.

"Scotty, it really has been a pleasure to have your company this year at National. The things we talked about were partially things that I have verbalized in the past and some things that I had never discussed. It was interesting to sound them out. I really appreciated your ear."

Wow! He appreciated my ear?

"Mr. O'Brien, no way. I can't tell you what this summer has meant to me. You changed my whole perspective on life. There's just no way to thank you. No way." I was almost getting choked up.

"Mr. O'Brien, I have got to ask you one more question. I don't know if I can phrase it right but I've got to try. I guess the simple question is 'why?' Why did you do the things you did, pursue the goals you pursued? What makes you tick? Why not just take the path of least resistance?"

"Scotty, that is one doozy of a question. I don't think anyone has ever asked me to justify the path I've taken. I've never really spent any time dwelling on this subject. Give me a second to think on it. What'll you have to drink?"

"Coke sounds great."

"How about a cheeseburger to go with it?"

"Sure. Thanks."

"Bobby, two cheeseburgers with fries and two Cokes. Well, first, as a child, I was much more aggressive than my older brother or my peers, for that matter. Much more willing to go into the breach. This is going clear back to age four or five, so there is probably some hereditary or personality factor at work. Aside from that, I really believe the primary motivational factors in my life were environmental.

"I'm going to go into a few negative experiences but let me remind you there have always been many, many more positives. If you remember black balls and white balls, I guess I would have it no other way. These experiences are like little movies or vignettes that I could always pull up if I needed them. For the most part, I suppressed them because they didn't have value unless I meant them to have value.

"One scene I remember is pulling cockleburs on my grandfather's farm on my hands and knees at a penny per 100 because the war was on and we were the poor country cousins who needed to make some money. And I can never forget my cousin Freddy from Ottawa, Kansas, driving up in his father's Oldsmobile eating an ice cream cone. I can remember the burning humiliation of that moment.

"I can remember a time when I very badly wanted a Red Rider BB gun for Christmas. I was consumed, selfishly so, with a desire for that Red Rider BB gun. Well, somehow my mother and father, who were great people, saw to it that on Christmas morning I had that Red Rider BB gun. But it was heartbreaking for me to notice that my mother's present was a box of chocolate-covered cherries from the Katz Drug Store.

"I remember my first formal dances in high school. There were two in those days, the prom and my girlfriend's sorority formal. I had bought her a gardenia corsage for the first one on Friday night but didn't have enough money to buy her a second one and I told her so. I could tell she understood, but it was still a real disappointment because it would be embarrassing to her — it would be hard for her to show up with the same corsage because none of her friends would. So I went to the florist and somehow got him to give me a cheap carnation corsage and I spent the next month running errands for him to pay for it.

"I remember very vividly that the battery in our family car, which I drove some, didn't work for at least two or three years. The battery was kaput but it never dawned on us to go buy a battery because that wasn't a part of our mental makeup. My dad would park it on a hill near our home and when we wanted to go anywhere, we would coast down the hill and jump start it. If it didn't start, my brothers and I would push it down Prospect Avenue as fast and long as we had to until my dad could get it started.

"I remember the prom my junior year in high school. It must have been during a time I was really growing. I didn't wear a coat or tie much in those days — like never. It was always jeans and leather jackets. I put on the only sport coat and slacks I had, didn't own a suit. The pants came up about four inches so that my ankles were not completely covered by my socks. The sport coat had the equivalent of three-quarter length sleeves. I looked like a clown. I ended up wearing one of my father's suits and that was equally absurd and very embarrassing.

"I remember later during my senior year, I took a college aptitude test and won a full tuition scholarship to either Yale or Stanford. My sister was on a full ride at the time to Wellesley College. There was no way for me to go to either Stanford or Yale because my scholarship was tuition only, not room and board. It was all my dad could do to scrape up enough money to send to my sister, to keep her in clothes and just general expenses so she didn't look like a complete fool. So I ended up at Baker in Baldwin near the wheat fields where I had picked cockleburs and lived with my grandparents in the same room. That wasn't embarrassing, it just wasn't Ivy League.

"These things built in me a very strong and literal inability to accept that life had to be that way. I remember thinking that I'd rather be a criminal — I thought I'd be a pretty good criminal — than endure the things I had seen, the things that had made grown men cry after the Depression. By the time I was six or seven, the remnants were still very visible. I saw that they would knock you down and not let you up. That's what I now call 'they shoot horses.'

"My solution for this state of things was to develop both consciously and instinctively an extreme sense of urgency — an almost angry urgency — an urgency that was not to be easily derailed. It included the development of my method of goal attainment and my concept of the competitive edge. Of course, I couldn't express them like I do now, but I instinctively felt the need to develop these tools. These were the things that I relied on. They nurtured me and I continued to refine them.

"To answer your question of why I did what I did or why I did it the way that I did, I am certain it wasn't for the money as much as it was to avoid the negative things that were unacceptable to me and to be avoided at any price. It became very clear to me during my early adulthood that people who didn't have this sense of urgency and this commitment were inevitably victims of chance — what I call flotsam — so they ended up wherever they might without a sense of having decided to go there."

Ouch. That struck a nerve. The inevitable victims of chance. That had been my path before this summer, but now I was resigned to create a path of my design and not to be governed by the winds of chance. Why was it that I had felt otherwise? Hadn't I believed in myself?

Suddenly I recognized myself in the mass of men leading lives of quiet desperation and I just wasn't going to go in their direction. I was going to just say no and wire my deal in a totally contrarian direction. Bob's speech had brought it all together for me. Without a compelling sense of direction and purpose, I was destined to be like most. Maybe lucky, maybe prosperous, hopefully happy, but reliant on the randomness of the path I just happened upon. I recognized Bob's need to define a path that took him in a particular direction. That direction had initially been away from something, but nevertheless it was a path of his choosing. As time and experience wisened him, his path became decidedly proactive and not reactive.

Bob glanced at his watch and moaned, "Jeez, Scotty, I'm sorry but I've got to run. I promised Mary Jo that we would have dinner with some of our friends tonight and then we're out of here in the morning."

I felt sick that I might never see Bob again.

"Listen, Scotty, let me give you my 800 number at the office. Give me a call sometime and tell me how you're doing, will ya?"

"Really, Mr. O'Brien? You wouldn't mind?"

"Really, I insist. Let me write my number on the back of this envelope."

He did and he handed me the envelope. It obviously had something in it. "Mr. O'Brien, there's something in here. Sure you don't need what's inside?"

"Oh, no, Scotty. That's yours."

"Mine?" I asked quizzically. And opened the envelope. There, to my utter disbelief, was a stack of $100 bills that seemed like an inch thick. "I can't accept this. No way. I've been stiffing you all summer."

"I know, Scotty. But remember the first time you did that, I said I was going to bet it in Vegas? Well, I did. And on the cruise ship. And at Monte Carlo. And at Vegas again. You know, I'm a pretty salty craps shooter."

I was stunned. I think I said something clever like, "I guess so."

"Yeah, I had a great run in Monte Carlo. I think you'll find $3,000 in there. Scotty, to my way of thinking, you earned it. I have really enjoyed the summer and I talked to you about a lot of things that I hadn't ever verbalized, at least not for a long time. I enjoyed watching you and George suck this stuff up and I can tell it made a difference. Hey, the money isn't mine. I just got lucky and parlayed that original $50 into three thou. I'd feel like I cheated you if you didn't take it."

I could not believe the man's generosity with his time and now this. "Bob, there is no way for me to repay you?"

"Oh, yes, there is. You can take what you've learned this summer and this dough and create a path that will take you where you want to go. And if you tell me about it, that will make this old war horse very happy."

I vowed to keep him posted every step of the way. And I did.

TODAY

The Circle is Unbroken

Years later, I had a conversation with Jorgen and he said that most people have snail-like antennae or receptors but, unlike a snail, they are generally rolled up in their heads. Only when those receptors are rolled out and red hot are we adaptable and capable of change. I guess my receptors were deployed that eventful summer at National more than 20 years ago.

My mentors that summer taught me about change and though at first I was totally resistant, I finally embraced adaptability as my mantra. It was my life raft as the world has become more chaotic with each passing year. Rapid change naturally brings about a feeling of loss of control and stability. Net result: unhappiness. It is interesting, but sad, to see the amount of energy dedicated to the opposing of change and the maintenance of the old ways. That same amount of energy applied to new initiatives would undoubtedly make those transitions smoother. I had decided that summer to go with the flow.

My mentors gifted me with wisdom. It wasn't knowledge or intellect. That was another truth revealed that summer. Wisdom has it all over intellect. I saw this exhibited time and time again at National. Those successful people were definitely bright, but they didn't exhibit high wattage as much as they knew what to say and how to say it. O'Brien, Ms. Falona, Jorgen, Case, Buck, Richard — what set them apart was their character and insights — not intellect. They could talk to anyone from the President of the United States to the shoeshine boy in the locker room. These people seemed to care about others and, in return, people really cared about them.

Another truth that applied to all my mentors that summer was their sense of responsibility. It was a cornerstone of every lesson and it has guided me since. If you associate with responsible individuals who keep their commitments, you'll be dealing with the "winners" of the world. Among the most admired people in the world are those who can be trusted and when they make a commitment, a promise, they will deliver no matter what the personal expense. You can't know enough people who, when they say "I'll do it," deliver.

Although Bob would try to minimize this, I have seen O'Brien put goal attainment and black balls/white balls to an incredible test over the past two years. Bob had an operation that placed electrodes in his spine to ease a condition that caused severe spasms of his neck muscles. The first operation failed, so a second operation was performed using a supposedly more appropriate device. When Bob awoke from the anesthetic after Operation #2, he found that he could not move anything on his left side. The surgery had left him paralyzed. I can't imagine the fear that would have hit my system at that moment but Bob dealt with it as if he had scripted it from his advice to me.

They immediately took him back to the operating room to pull the leads out of the electrical device they had implanted. He had gone in for an operation to correct a neck problem and had wound up paralyzed. Fortunately, the second operation of the day returned some mobility to his left side. Then came a period of wait-and-see to assess the damage. The good news was he was not paralyzed but nevertheless faced considerable rehab.

Man, what a black ball to be dealt. He attacked the problem in his usual way — with intensity and with a sense of humor. Of course he was outraged, but he was not going to let those negative emotions interfere with the task at hand, getting back to where he was before the operation. I visited him after a month of physical therapy and he was back to about 50 percent on his left side. I asked him what had been revealed by his ordeal.

He told me the following, "What this has done is simply call upon some of the things we've talked about over the years. Particularly WILL. The word perseverance doesn't do it justice. It has brought forth the need, the absolute need, to endure and to make a commitment and void all thoughts except the completion of the task. There is no time for 'Why me?' Scotty, my options were reduced to two: Curl up in a ball and literally waste away or don't look back and move ahead.

"This was a huge black ball that came at me, not like a lost sale or anything so trivial. This was a constant black ball that loomed like a serpent looking for a way to seep through my defenses and smack me down. So the trick is to be ever vigilant and not to hold that black ball out there. I kept it away in several ways. One was just pure meanness on my part. I was not going to let the incompetence of these doctors rob me of the quality of my life. I was going to get that playing field back to even. They had taken me to the depths of indignity. Now I am not sure what I am going to do when I get back to the level field, but it is propelling me. The other method I have employed to keep the black ball away is the Satchel Paige saying of 'Don't look back, somebody may be gaining on you.' A third method I have used is sort of comparative. No matter how bad I felt about my plight, while I was around the hospital I saw people who had no options. They did not have the option of getting to the level playing field. They had no control over their destiny because they were dreadfully sick. I had it in my power to get well and it was thereby reduced to an inconvenience. I could deal with that. It was within my control to gain back the strength and coordination of my body. I knew a lot of people in those hospitals would gladly change places with me."

That summer at National I found the greatest teachers of my life. Now I really want to take you full circle. I am no longer just an ex-caddie of National. I am a full-fledged member there and I can honestly say that without my experience as a caddie, I would never have become a member. Because I was ready to learn, my mentors began the process of filling my empty vessel. I was transformed from a kid who thought he had it pretty well figured out into a young man who knew he had a tremendous amount to learn. I remember one of my mentors telling me that I was a "most dangerous man." He said, "The most dangerous man is the man who doesn't know what he doesn't know."

When I got past that, I was able to start my ascent towards wisdom. But the key was having a mentor, someone I could talk to, ask stupid questions of, bounce ideas off of without fear that I would be considered idiotic. A mentor who was willing to share his wisdom. Once I opened my eyes to this method of learning, I could fly by my peers. It was just a matter of time after that.

Well, that concludes the tale of my summer at National and the lessons I took away with me. Today, I am playing with another member whom you met earlier, George Spachmann. George hit it huge in the computer field. He created a way of selling data processing services and expertise on a contract basis. He has his own jet and credits his success to the think tank we created at NuWay that summer.

He kept his notes on all of this in his computer, including the sheet on leadership. He created workshops in his company on many of those topics. In fact, the first thing all of his new employees go through is a seminar on Goal Attainment. He says the results are unbelievable.

George and I have vowed to identify a caddie this summer whom we can torment with life's great secrets like Bob did for us. We both hope that our "victim" will stiff us the way I did. Richard has retired so we can't depend on him to set us up with our "Scotty," but we did have a looper yesterday who seemed to think he knew everything. George and I think he might be a good project. There's also a young lady from the nearby state university. Her name is Carly. I think she would really like to hear about my days as a caddie at National.

"Hi, Carly. My name is David Scott. My friends call me Scotty. I wish you would too. What brings you to National? What are you studying? You say you're on the golf team?"

Find out what happens with Scotty in...

RATTLE THE CUP

due out in 1998

Bob O'Byrne is Chairman of Robert
O'Byrne and Associates, an employee
benefits company. Founded in 1962,
the company has grown to 150 employees in fourteen offices across the country and was named the 1995 Small
Business of the Year by the Kansas City
Chamber of Commerce. Bob has been
recognized as one of the Outstanding
Alumni of the Bloch School of Business
(University of Missouri, Kansas City).

Gary Abram is president of Partners Group a national executive search company located in Kansas City specializing in the insurance industry. He taught and coached at the high school and college level, worked in the insurance industry and, in the days before free agents, was a professional baseball player.

There are two aspects of *Distance to the Green* that I really appreciated. First, the business philosophy is really valuable and is delivered in a most entertaining way. Secondly, some of my most memorable and rewarding experiences have been as mentor and as protégé. The development of the O'Brien and Scotty relationship is terrific. I look forward to their next book to find out what happens to both.

Rick Darnaby, President of Nutrasweet
Corporate VP/Global Brand Management-Motorola

What a great book! I am reminded that there are no new truths — just life's lessons passed on to others. I am going to share this with my 15-year-old son.

Alan Mauch
Executive Vice President, Employers Reinsurance Corporation

Distance to the Green offers both straightforward and valuable techniques for goal attainment...The lessons ring true not only for anyone starting a new career, but also for anyone who wishes to become more effective and successful. I just wish my putting was as sound as the messages in the book.

Howard E. Jones, Management Consultant
Vice President, Hallmark Cards, Inc. (retired)

This delightful story, set on a golf course, is an instructive and thought-provoking read on some of life's deeper challenges: figuring out where you really want to go and finding the path that will get you there.

Lee Bolman
Henry R. Bloch Leadership Chair, U.of Missouri-Kansas City
Co-author with Terrence Deal, "Leading with Soul"

...it is apparent that the Business World can be offered a great and most comprehensive business learning atmosphere while at the same time enjoy the pleasures of playing and sharing the friendly competition in the best of all games...Golf! You have a winner...

Jon E. Jacobson
Executive Director/CEO Midwest Section PGA